"HOW DID YOU GET HERE?"

One Black Man's Journey through White Corporate
America

William T. Parker

PAP Publishers, LLC

Atlanta, Georgia

Dedication

Lisa Parker Mackay, whose love and intelligence continue to help me frame thoughts about my life.

To my other children, Jefferson, Gregory, and Jason, to my precocious grandchildren, all of whom have the "audacious gene," which makes me know that they will find the road less traveled.

To the many teachers, friends, lovers, and colleagues who have assisted in smoothing my path while understanding that I always saw a different way.

To my wonderful wife, Phyllis, who understands the passion that I have for writing and tolerates the many hours that I spend doing what I love.

Thanks to you all and I dedicate this book to you with love.

WTP, February, 2015

PREFACE

We all go through life being helped by many different people. We don't always remember to thank them at the time, and sometimes we wait until it's too late. Sometimes we don't even recognize the importance of these people to our lives until years later. A number of people have filled my life with unspeakable joy, and too many times my recognition of their contribution didn't come until years after the fact.

This book, which represents my story, includes references to many of these people, most of whom have helped to define who I am today. I lovingly dedicate this book to each one of you. As you read through these pages, I hope you will recognize yourselves and the great influences you had on me during my journey.

Someone once said that everyone's life is shaped by 10 defining moments, seven critical choices, and eight pivotal people. I may not have identified all of the moments, choices, or people, but I have endeavored to the best of my recollection to acknowledge them all in these pages. Some merit special attention. These special individuals are Sophie Mason, whose quiet and gentle sprit gave me the idea for this book, J. Peter Conway, my first real mentor on my corporate journey; and Charles H. "Chip" Siegel, a great friend and generous person.

Last but not least, The Achievers, a group of wonderful Black men who have been nothing short of a band of brothers through the last quarter century of my life.

TABLE OF CONTENTS

INTRODUCTION

This book is a personal story and not a treatise on the state of racism in America, even though that is an integral part of the theme throughout the book.

This book is not designed to espouse any particular point of view. It is simply a recounting of my personal experiences and obstacles encountered in my quest to participate in the American dream. I invite you to draw your own conclusions about the historical or current state of race relations in the United States and how you may or may not relate. I confess, however, that my personal philosophy is to see that every person who I encounter—either in business or my personal life—is better because of the experience.

This story has been in my head for over 30 years. I finally decided to bring it to life because of a series of recent events. It was time to get the story out of my head and on to paper.

In the summer of 2011, I attended a gathering of associates (all were White, which was not unusual). I don't remember the specifics of the particular conversation, but ultimately the discussion turned to me. I was asked, essentially, to talk about my background and career. It has been my personal experience that White people always seem curious about how Black people end up in places and situations they deem uncharacteristic, given the racial undertones that still exist in this country.

Sophie Mason, one of the gatherers, asked if I would be willing to tell my story to the Midtown Atlanta Rotary Club. Sophie believed that the subject of race in America was more often than not ignored, and most of the time it appeared to be an issue that White people felt much too uncomfortable to contemplate or discuss with transparency. Knowing this belief, I agreed to make the presentation and, as a result of that experience, I decided to expand that speech into a book.

For many years, my thinking was that White people were afraid to discuss the issue of race in a serious fashion, and I was not really sure of the reason why this was so. Now, however, I believe that people who have not had to experience the effects and subtleties of racism in the United States really don't believe that a racial problem exists. They cannot fathom themselves as "racist" and I agree that, for the most part, they are not racist.

I believe that for a person to be consciously racist, his or her thinking requires a degree of insanity that most functioning humans cannot manage and still function properly.

Therefore, I think that over a number of generations, White people have constructed this society in such a manner as to institutionalize the facts of racist behavior. Thanks to their efforts, racist behavior no longer requires much if any conscious thought. It simply happens during the course of the normal, everyday functioning of society.

For example, I was having lunch one day with a colleague. This gentlemen was a vice president of a major insurance company. During the course of our meal, he broached the subject of racism in the South in general and in Atlanta in particular. His issue was that he believed "the situation had improved" in recent years and he wondered whether I agreed. I questioned him on the status of race relations within his company, and he assured me that their organization was one of the most diverse in the city. In fact, I believe he indicated that more than 40% of their employees were minorities. My next question was, "Then how many of those employees are represented in field sales and management positions?"

After a few moments of contemplation, he said "None." I was shocked because I knew that this man's company employed a large number of people in the Atlanta area. It turns out that all of their minority employees were in non-customer-facing positions. I indicated to the man that this arrangement was a clear indication of institutional racism, which had developed over a period of time and had become the normal manner of thinking for management in his company. The executives automatically believed that persons of color could not represent the company in the marketplace. He admitted that the thought of representation by persons of color had not occurred to him until we had our conversation. He had assumed that the company's policies and practices were outstanding, until the reality of how corporate America actually works was presented to him in living color, as it were.

Recent surveys by reputable organizations such as the Pew Foundation and others indicate that a majority of White Americans do not see situations of this nature in the context of racism or racist behavior, which serves to validate my contention that thoughts of this nature are just a part of the normal thinking and functioning processes of society. Most people don't think about how business structures of this type have an impact on people's lives. They don't think about how the functioning of the business itself is wasting valuable resources by foregoing the use of intellectual capital contained in the minds of employees who are excluded from full participation in all areas of the company simply because of the color of their skin.

The collective psyches of both Black and White people have been co-opted by this system of innate racism so that everyone is supposed to maintain his or her place in the hierarchy without question. While most people are willing to accept this premise as truth, there are many free-thinking individuals on both sides of the divide who recognize that there can be a different way.

Much of my story fits into this same pattern. As I made my journey through White corporate America, I was often confronted by the same institutionalized thinking. Fortunately, I had the fortitude to withstand the often seemingly overwhelming onslaught. There were several occasions when the companies I worked for were led by individuals who refused to look beyond their own racist feelings. These companies miss significant new business and profit opportunities, sometimes reaching into hundreds of millions of dollars.

By sharing these stories about my life and experiences, I hope to stimulate some discussion about the real costs of racism and racist behavior. I want to encourage people to take a hard look at how racist feeling and practices have an impact in their lives—not just on the lives of victims, but also on those of perpetrators of racism. This impact is psychological and economic, perhaps in ways that we don't even recognize.

When I started this recollection, I struggled with the subtitle of this book. "Sojourn" seemed appropriate to describe how I began my climb up the American corporate ladder, but a sojourn is temporary. "Trek" came to mind because that's what it has really felt like, but "journey"—that was it! Journey means to travel for a long time, and that was the most accurate description of my life in corporate America, which began in 1965.

At the beginning of my adult life, my dream was to work for a major American corporation as a top-level executive. During the course of my career, I successfully landed positions with three different major companies. The year 1965 was a pivotal time for Black Americans. The Civil Rights Act, passed in 1964, was intended to ban discrimination in the workplace and end legalized segregation.

In 1965, I was the third Black professional employee hired by Union Carbide Corporation. From there, I moved on to Eastman Kodak Company, and finally to E & J Gallo Winery. Union Carbide no longer exists as a business entity and Eastman Kodak Company is but a shadow of its former self. E & J Gallo Winery, however, continues to thrive and lead its industry as the largest winery in the world after 83 years.

I believe E & J Gallo Winery's longevity comes from the open-mindedness of its management and the vision of its founders who, in my experience, refused to tolerate or condone racist ideologies or attitudes within the ranks of the organization.

CHAPTER ONE

The Beginning

I was born in Wilson, North Carolina, during the summer of 1943. Wilson is a small town in the coastal plain region of the state. During my childhood, Wilson was in the heart of tobacco country.

My grandfather, Thomas Parker, was the only child of Elizabeth Bennett, who was born in about 1867 in Nash County, North Carolina. Elizabeth was the "free born" daughter of a former slave named Richard Parker. My grandmother, Emma Dew Parker, and her brother, Claude Dew, were the bastard children of a White farmer named Warren Ellis. My grandparents were sharecroppers who had 10 children: Sylvester, Elizabeth, Jesse, Edith, William Eugene, Arthur Lee, Dorothy, Esther, Claude and Inez.

My father, Jesse, was the third of the 10 children. Three of my grandparents' sons served in World War II. Jesse and Eugene served in the

Army in Europe, while Arthur Lee served in the Navy in the Pacific.

My mother was Mamie Fuller of Fayetteville, North Carolina, daughter of Lillie and Noah Fuller. While I never heard their story during my parents' lifetimes, I was later told that they met in Washington, DC, in 1942. They were married in Baltimore and, soon after, my dad was drafted into the Army. My mother was pregnant with me at the time and went to live with my paternal grandparents in Elm City, North Carolina, near Wilson.

I was the first Parker grandson born into the family and was honored to carry on the family name. There were, in fact, three other older grandchildren born to Elizabeth, but because they were not named "Parker," the legacy fell to me.

My mother and I lived with my grandparents until 1945, when my dad came home from the war. My most vivid memories of those very early years are of my Grandma Emma. I bonded with her almost completely (even more so than with my mother). I felt protected in her arms and in her presence. Tragedy struck in early 1946, when she died rather suddenly from leukemia at the age of 51. Honestly, I didn't fully recover from this loss until I was about 40 years old.

My sister Delores was born in September, 1946. That same year, we moved to Elvie Street in

Wilson, North Carolina, where my younger sister, Jessie Gray, was born in 1949. We lived on Elvie Street until I left for college.

In our early years, Delores and I spent summers with our maternal grandmother, Lillie Fuller, and with my mother's older sister, Louella Williams, in Fayetteville, North Carolina. The last summer we spent in Fayetteville was 1949, the year our younger sister was born. As children, we didn't even know that our mom was expecting another child.

I started kindergarten at St. Alphonsus Catholic School in 1948. St. Alphonsus provided a wonderful educational foundation and learning experience. I made several lifelong friends there. For the first 2 years of my educational career, I traveled to school by taxi. My parents didn't own a car and, even after they'd bought a car, my mother never learned to drive.

I was an adventurous kid. On my first day of school, I decided not to wait for the taxi—I walked home! I made this decision primarily because the other kids, including my new best friend, Jimmy Washington, were walking home. Jimmy Washington lived two blocks away from school. I lived about 4 miles away and probably had no idea about how to get home, but everyone else was walking, so I just joined the parade. In truth, I'm not really sure if I even thought about the fact that I didn't know how to get home.

I still don't remember exactly how it happened, but I ended up about 2 miles away from school. I was completely lost and crying like the average 5-year-old kid who had no idea where he is or how to get to where he wants to be. If it hadn't been for Mrs. Narcissus Townsend, one of my father's coworkers, who recognized me and put me in a taxi, I'm not sure whether or how I would have ever gotten home. That little experience took care of my walking home adventures for a while.

Beginning in second grade, I left school at the end of the day and walked to the public library downtown, which was about half a mile away. The library was a storefront facility for Black folks in Wilson in the late 1940s and early 1950s.

At the library, I read books and talked to the librarians while I waited for my father, who worked nearby, to pick me up for the trip home. I think that the ladies who worked at the library were fascinated with me because, even at that age, I was an avid reader and had developed the surprisingly good skill of storytelling. I was able to talk to them on a mature level about what I was reading and what I was learning in school, just two adults chatting with each other while one of us waited for his father to walk him home.

The librarians guided my reading and plied me with wonderful books to encourage my continued interest and skills. To this day, I read on average two books per month, with sometimes as many as

10 books in progress at any given time. This early exposure to books piqued my interest in learning and my desire to achieve greatness as an adult.

On some afternoons, rather than go to the library, I'd take a detour to the Ritz Theater, a Black-owned movie house in Wilson. The price of admission was 10₵. I always had to sit in the back row by the door so the ticket taker could keep an eye on me while I waited for my dad. My favorite afternoons, though, were the ones I spent at the library.

By the time I reached the third grade, I started to walk to school on my own; mind you, I was always accompanied by high school kids from the neighborhood who were walking in the same direction. I like to think they thought of me as something akin to a little brother, although I never asked. Some of them might have thought, at first, that I was attending high school.

These were really good times for us. My dad worked in dry cleaning for Wardrobe Cleaners, a Black-owned business in the Black business district of downtown Wilson. Later, he worked for Hargett Cleaners, another Black-owned firm across the street.

In the 1940s and 1950s, Wilson had a thriving Black middle class, as did most Southern cities in the days prior to integration. The Black business district in Wilson was home to two drycleaners, two drug stores, a movie theater, restaurant, several clothing stores, barber shops, beauty salons, and a beauty school. There were also two Black doctors in town and two dentists. My father was a bootlegger; nowadays, he'd probably be considered a small-time drug dealer, so life for our family was really good. We were one of the few families on our street who owned their own home. Home ownership was rare for Black people in the late '40s and '50s in Wilson. In addition to being a bootlegger, my dad had a full-time job.

I discovered through conversations with my dad that he had learned the trades of tailoring and dry cleaning in the Army. It wasn't until much later that I learned that Black soldiers had been relegated to the service areas of the military and were usually not assigned to combat brigades. Many of my father's friends who had served in the Army during World War II were tradesmen—electricians, carpenters, coopers, and so on. On a positive note, they could earn a good living after their military stints. I suspect that many of them would not have had those skills were it not for their military service.

My father always said that he wanted to be a doctor, but he only had a sixth-grade education and, following World War II, he was not allowed to participate in the benefits offered under the G.I. Bill or the veterans' benefits for housing that were readily available to White veterans of the war. His dream then became that his children would be educated to the fullest extent possible.

Although I started my educational career at Saint Alphonsus Catholic School, it was quite expensive. It was the best school available for Black kids at that time, but I was only able to attend through the third grade. In 1951, our family's financial security took a major hit: my dad was arrested for bootlegging and was sent to prison for 1 year and 1 day, the standard sentence for Black bootleggers. I later discovered that White bootleggers were usually sentenced to a period of 11 months and 3 days. I don't know many of the details—I was just a child and, even after my father returned from prison, the matter was simply never discussed by anyone in the family. That same year, a new public school began construction in our neighborhood. In, 1953 Elvie Street Elementary School opened, just one block away from my house. Because it was in the neighborhood and was a free public school, I attended that school from the fourth grade through sixth grade

My experiences at Elvie Street School were dramatically different from those at Saint Alphonsus. I met new kids and most of them were poor. In retrospect, I'm sure that we were poor, too, but I didn't have that perception at the time. The teachers at the Elvie Street School treated me as "the responsible child."

During my 3 years at Elvie Street Elementary School, I managed to get into trouble several times for what I now recognize as childish pranks. At the time, though, I was just a child having fun and playing. I was scolded for infractions such as riding the folding chair racks across the gym floor. I was repeatedly told that they "expected much better of me." I wondered why I couldn't just be a kid like everyone else and just have some fun. Now I realize the teachers believed I was more mature than most of my peers and that I could be relied upon to set a good example.

In retrospect, I think that my teachers were trying to instill in me a sense of responsibility, but the lesson didn't resonate well at the time. I still harbor personal resentment, sometimes, for feeling the need to be the responsible one in the group, the example for everyone to follow. I don't think they knew about the personal tragedy unfolding in my young life.

My academic experience at Elvie Street Elementary School was, by and large, a good one. I was a smart kid and made friends easily. I got along well with everyone. I was even made captain of the school safety patrol, a position of honor, but one which I did not particularly enjoy. I thought it prevented me from enjoying the fun stuff that kids really liked to do, such as riding the chair racks across the gym floor! It was also about this time that I remember several kids in the neighborhood and at school occasionally commenting that I was "different." I didn't understand what they meant, but as a kid, being thought of as different is not a good thing. I overheard the same comment from teachers. I heard that same comment many times as I was growing up, and well into my adulthood.

My parents divorced in early 1953 and my mother left us with my father. I don't remember much about the events leading up to the split; in our family, the divorce was yet another elephant in the room. It was never discussed, and it marked the beginning of a particularly difficult time in the lives of my sisters and in mine. My most vivid memory is one of constantly thinking that I didn't know what I would find for myself in the world when I became a grown-up, but I knew that it had to be better than the life we were living then. After the divorce, we didn't get to see our mother for almost 2 years, other than for a brief period during Christmas in 1954.

When my parents divorced, I was given primary responsible for taking care of my two sisters, who were 5 and 2 years old at the time. It wasn't so much that I was "given" responsibility, but there was no one else to care for them but me. These were very dark days for us. We rarely got to see my father in person. Sometimes we would go as long as 2 weeks without actually seeing him, but there was evidence that he had been in the house.

Sometimes, I'd notice things had been moved around in the kitchen and food had been left for us to eat. I suspected my father came in late and left early in the mornings, before we were awake.

Although my dad owned our house, which was indeed a rarity at that time, it was not a very good house. It was your basic shotgun house—typical of the era and common for Black folks. The house had three rooms with an enclosed toilet on the back porch, making it slightly more tolerable. The house was heated with a coal-burning stove, and a fire had to be started each morning to warm up the house so we could get ready for school. Starting and feeding the fire was another task left to me because my dad wasn't there and didn't start the fire before he left for work. We also had a kerosene cooking stove in the kitchen, and as one might imagine, this combination of fire sources was a recipe for disaster. One morning while trying to get the house heated so my sisters could get dressed in some degree of warmth and heat some water for oatmeal, I lit the kerosene stove. The water boiled over and the result was a kitchen fire that did a great deal of damage to the entire house. I managed to get the girls out of the house partially dressed and summoned the fire department. Most of the house was saved, but the roof and kitchen sustained major fire damage.

The remainder of the house suffered primarily smoke and water damage. The situation being what it was, we had no choice but to live in the damaged house for several weeks while it was being repaired. Thankfully, my dad had insurance.

This experience left an indelible mark on my psyche. I vowed that my children would never have to put their feet on a cold floor. This childhood promise to myself proved difficult to keep, only because I acquired some affluence and purchased a house with hardwood floors in the bedrooms, but I made sure that my children always had rugs at their bedsides.

CHAPTER TWO

NEW HAVEN, 1955

In the summer of 1955, several months after my dad had started his new business, my mother came home and announced to my father that she wanted my sisters and me to live with her in Connecticut. No one ever discussed this option with my sisters and me, or even asked what we thought about this change in our lives. It just happened. We moved to New Haven. I was excited about the possibility of leaving Wilson. I was anxious to see what the world was like beyond our little home town.

I remember the train ride to New Haven quite clearly, especially the stop in New York City and the Grand Central Terminal. Grand Central was the largest building that I had ever seen. The impression it made me on as a child remains with me as an adult.

That fall, I was enrolled in the seventh grade at Troup Junior High School on Edgewood Avenue in New Haven. Seventh grade marked my first real encounter with White people.

We were only in New Haven for a few months, primarily because my mother worked as a domestic and she only earned $50 a week. She simply couldn't afford to keep us with her and maintain her own life.

I don't know if she received any money from my father, but I suspect that she did not.

My sisters and I shared one room of an apartment with an older couple, Mr. and Mrs. King. I had a single bed and my sisters shared the other single bed. The Kings' apartment was on the second floor of a two-story home. Although I didn't realize it at the time, I now suspect it was a boarding house. Mrs. King owned the home at 112 Dwight Street with her sister. The house was about two blocks from the Yale Campus, which turned out to be a wonderful thing for me and my inquisitive mind.

My mother was a live-in domestic for a wealthy White family. Life with the Kings was very restrictive for us. We were only allowed to eat the food that our mother provided. As difficult as life was for me at the time, I'm sure it was much more so for my sisters because I managed to stay out of the house a good deal of the time. My sisters were much younger, so they were trapped and had to endure watching television in Mrs. King's sister's apartment and going to church with them— Daddy Grace's House of Prayer.

I recall my time in New Haven as being filled with lots of interesting experiences. I discovered the YMCA, something that didn't exist for Black people in Wilson. Sometimes I went swimming there. I was never a particularly good swimmer, but poor ability didn't keep me from trying. Later that school year, I joined the swim club at school, which met at the Y, but because I wasn't a good swimmer, this scheme didn't work out very well. I almost drowned the first time I jumped in the deep end of the pool and had to be rescued by the lifeguard.

Even though I was only 11 years old, I was a big kid. Perhaps because of all the responsibility I had had growing up to that point, I was mature for my age. As such, I was able to get around without much interference during the 7 months my sisters and I lived in New Haven. Most people who didn't know me thought that I was 18 years old! I made the most of the opportunity and spent my free time exploring the city and the Yale campus. I attended several Yale football games, pretended to be a student at Yale, I got a job working at the YMCA bowling alley as a pin setter. Remember if you will that this time was long before the days of automatic pin setters! My job was to manually reset the pins after each bowler had completed his turn. I don't think I did a particularly good job of setting pins, but the manager didn't have anyone else to do it, so I didn't get fired. The pay was only 10¢ per frame bowled and the typical game took about 30 minutes, with most people bowling about three games.

It might not seem like much now, but on average, I earned about $3 per day and I could usually work about 3 days per week. For Christmas that year, I got my mother to help me buy my first watch, a Boluva. The watch cost $49 and I paid for it at the rate of $1 per week. Setting pins afforded me freedom and independence that would have been out of reach without that job. That job also made me painfully aware at an early age that I would be useless as a manual laborer.

My brief time at Troup Junior High School was interesting and enlightening. Miss Grace Madden was my home room and math teacher. She was, as I remember, what would have been called an "old maid" school marm. Miss Madden was probably in her 60s at the time, but was a wonderful teacher. I was a good student at Troup, but we were living with the Kings, and with my mother trying to support us on her meager earnings, supplemented by my $9 week from the bowling alley, we were surely poor, even though I still didn't recognize myself as poor. I guess that poverty really is just a state of mind. I can remember being treated differently by the teachers here, too. I recognized this treatment but I didn't understand why. All of my teachers were White, so when I think about it now, the best explanation I can come up with is that I was a good student and poor and they wanted to help in any way possible.

Prior to landing my wonderful job at the bowling alley, my music teacher would give me 25¢ if I asked him for it. I would use the money to buy lunch in the school cafeteria. Some days, he would offer the money without my having to ask, probably sensing that I had not eaten much since lunch the day before. He introduced me to classical music, which he played often in class. He taught us how to handle the precious records—music was recorded on vinyl discs in the old days—when we placed them on the player. Keeping the records clean was important to prevent the sound quality from being distorted. I still remember and follow those lessons, and to this day, I am still a devoted fan of classical music.

Another experience I remember from my time at Troup Junior High School was being harassed by the other Black kids. I surmised that it was because I was a Southerner. I didn't really have to do much surmising because they told me that was their reason. The Black kids weren't interested in having me as their friend, so I made friends with the White kids, most notably, Paul Valenti, with whom I developed a real friendship, and Michael Wacks, whose father owned a hardware store about a block from where we lived on Dwight Street. I was friendly with several other classmates, but none of them blossomed into real friendships beyond Paul and Michael. I regret not doing more to maintain those friendships over the years.

I spent a lot of time at the home of an associate of my mother, Mrs. Gladys Wilson, who lived across the street from Troup Junior High School. Her son Patrick was a year older than me. I'm reluctant to say that Patrick and I were friends. I think it was more that I just hung on because I didn't know anyone else my own age, and Patrick allowed me to hang around.

Mrs. Wilson was never particularly friendly to me; in fact, she was often outright hostile. I recall her telling me frequently, "You will never amount to anything," and that I smelled bad. I must admit, after my experiences with my own teenage sons, I can agree my hygiene was probably not the best, but I always rejected her notion that I wouldn't amount to anything. Perhaps her prediction of failure spurred me to try harder to make something of myself. I knew that I was intellectually gifted, certainly more so than her son, and I was certain that I would achieve the lofty goals I would set for myself. I often wondered whether she said these things because she recognized that I was significantly smarter than her son, Patrick.

While in New Haven, I also met and spent a great deal of time with a young couple, George and Julia, who rented an apartment at the Wilson house. George was in the U.S. Air Force and was attending Yale University, studying Japanese in preparation for deployment to Japan. I wasn't sure if they thought that I was an interesting kid or just a royal pain, but I loved being around them and talking about whatever subject came to mind—and they didn't seem to mind spending time talking with me.

One Sunday in December 1955, my mother got George to drive us to visit my uncle Lemon Fuller, her eldest brother. Uncle Lemon lived in Newark, New Jersey. My strongest memory of that visit is that Uncle Lemon lived in a rundown tenement house. I was particularly shocked by this discovery because the stories my mother's family had always told indicated that Lemon was the most successful member of the Fuller family, having moved to New Jersey years earlier to make his fortune.

Uncle Lemon didn't leave me with a very good impression of his good life. By this time in my own life, I had already seen the city lights of New York and New Haven. Life in a tenement in Newark was for damn sure not my idea of success. I knew I wanted more. I always did.

Later on, Uncle Lemon built a small house in his hometown, Fayetteville, North Carolina. That became his retirement home. I visited him once or twice at that house in his older years. Uncle Lemon died at age 96 in the mid-1980s.

While in New Haven, I got to visit my mother at her place of employment on some weekends. She worked for Walter Sheahan, Jr... The Sheahan family lived on The Villa Rosa in Milford, Connecticut. When these visits were allowed and possible, money being tight, as you will recall—I certainly do—I would take the bus to Milford to see my mother.

The Sheahan's house was a large year-round beach house in which they lived with their two children and a dog named Casey. I remember the dog quite clearly. Casey was a German shepherd who tried to bite me at our first meeting; he missed my flesh, but tore a small hole in my pants. It's little wonder I still harbor a certain reluctance toward dogs. This mishap turned out to be a fortunate event, however; because of my encounter with Casey, I got to meet Walter Sheahan, Sr., the CEO of New England Iron Works.

He was at his summer home, which was two doors away on The Villa Rosa. When he heard Casey's assault of my leg, he asked for me to come over so he could inspect the damage to my pants. I think that he paid my mother about $10 for the damage, which was probably more than the pants cost when she first bought them. I remember that he was eating breakfast and asked me if I wanted to join him, and I did. We had a wide-ranging conversation about school and what I liked to do. He was also reading *The New York Times* and saw that I was interested in the newspaper, so we had a brief conversation about one of the issues of the day.

It's possible he might have just wanted to relax and get rid of me, but from my perspective, I had made a new friend. I was always interested in talking to adults, and I genuinely think he enjoyed our brief time together that morning.

The reason I think Mr. Sheahan was my friend is that he decided, soon after my little encounter with Casey, that it would be a good idea for me to learn how to fish. I had never been fishing. He personally took on the task of teaching me how to fish. Much to his chagrin, he thought it would keep me occupied so he could relax, but no such luck. All I wanted to do was talk and listen to stories. When Mr. Sheahan took me fishing, I caught an eel. I was sure it was a snake, and no amount of convincing by the experienced angler would convince me otherwise. The fishing adventure was over for that day.

That fishing adventure was my first opportunity to see how really wealthy White people lived. I knew right away that this was the life to which I aspired. I later learned that Mr. Sheahan, Sr., died in 1958, three years after we met, but that was probably one of the 10 defining moments of my life. I did not recognize it at the time, but that encounter had a profound and lasting impact.

My sisters and I lived in New Haven until March 1956, when we went back to Wilson because Mom couldn't afford to keep us any longer. Even though we were there for less than a year, my life had changed immeasurably. I had seen the skyscrapers of New York and been to Grand Central Station. I had walked on the campus of Yale University, and had visited as a guest—at least in my mind—the homes of some of the wealthiest White people in the country and they had not been hostile toward me.

I had one other experience with New Haven about a year later. My mother had left the Sheahan's and was living with some friends when I went for a 2-week visit. I stayed at the YMCA for the first week and then had to leave because I didn't have any more money for rent. While I didn't know it beforehand, my mother had apparently been relying on me to get a job.

After having to leave the YMCA, I went to Stamford, where I spent a week sleeping on the couch at the apartment of another friend of my mother.

I tried to find a job in Stamford with the idea of at least staying for the summer. One day, I called a local restaurant that had placed a help wanted ad in the local paper. I was told that they were very busy and that they were hiring. I insisted on speaking to the manager, but the person on the phone said that it was not necessary. He said that the restaurant was "hiring everybody, so just come on out."

The regular bus fare in Stamford at the time was 15¢ each way, and 15¢ was literally all the money I had in the world at that time, but I was so confident, based on the phone call, that I would get the job, so off I went to the restaurant.

The restaurant location was actually beyond the end of the bus line and, when the bus reached the end of its run, the driver informed me that the fare was 25¢ and not the 15¢ I had thought it would be. I did not have the extra dime, so the driver accused me of being a deadbeat and told me to get off the bus. I paid the fifteen cents and promptly departed, shaken but still confident that I would be hired. I was unconcerned about where and how I would get the money for the return trip.

I walked the rest of the way from the bus stop to the restaurant and asked to see the manager, who promptly advised me that he was not hiring and that I should leave. I protested and recounted the phone call that I had earlier with an employee, but he still insisted that he was not hiring and told me that I had to leave. I persisted, but he was adamant. He did not have any jobs for me.

As a last resort, I asked him for a glass of water and for 25¢ for the bus ride back into the city. It took a bit of begging, but finally he relented and gave me the water and the 25¢. I really didn't realize it at the time, but I had just experienced my first real encounter with blatant racial discrimination. Following this incident, I called my dad for money, which he sent and I returned to Wilson a few days later. I spent the remainder of my childhood in Wilson.

I have visited New Haven only once in the years since that time, and that was in 2002. I was driving my youngest son, Jefferson, to Boston to enroll him at MIT.

We stopped in New Haven and toured the places where I had spent a part of my childhood. Troup Junior High School was boarded up with a fence around the property. The house on Dwight Street was gone, replaced by a church parking lot. The Wilson's house was still there, but rundown, and the neighborhood overall had deteriorated.

CHAPTER THREE

Back to Wilson

My sisters and I got back to Wilson in February of 1956 and I enrolled in the seventh grade at Charles H. Darden High School. I remained at Darden until graduation in June 1961. High school was a positive experience for me. The school was blessed with some of the best teachers on the planet. I have discovered through my research in preparation for this book that almost 80% of the teachers at Darden High School during my tenure had advanced degrees from some of the nation's most prestigious universities. Several of them had master's degrees from schools such as Northwestern, University of Chicago, Columbia, and Boston University —African American teachers, mind you. They managed to keep us isolated in a cocoon-like environment, almost completely shielded from the racist experiences being heaped upon most Black people during that era.

In high school, we got to experience classical ballet, opera, symphonies, and plays presented at the Black universities and colleges in North Carolina. We were taught that we were the best and that we were expected to achieve greatness in our lives, not just for ourselves, but for others.

Our teachers were excellent, caring individuals. I got along well with my classmates. I continued to be told that I was different, and I still didn't feel comfortable wearing this label.

You can't imagine how many times I've heard people say to me, "You're different." I think I am only now beginning to understand and internalize this difference as something positive. I grew to understand that I was being referred to as a different kind of thinker, which made sense, because I have always been a person who did not accept the norm as my lot in life, or as something I needed to just live with.

I always thought that I could achieve anything I set my mind to achieving. I never perceived that race was a barrier. I always knew that I could transcend notions of limitations and go beyond them. I was creative and curious from a very young age. I was always a learner and thinker.

The members of the Charles H. Darden High School class of 1961 have succeeded disproportionately well for a group of Black kids from Wilson, North Carolina. My schoolmates have gone on to achieve positions such as a seat in the U.S. Congress, first Black Supreme Court judge in North Carolina, and first Black district attorney in North Carolina.

One classmate attended Wellesley College—an exclusive women's college—and later became principal of Philadelphia's Girls High School, the last all girls' public high school in the nation.

We had never heard of Wellesley at the time and we wondered how she managed to get there. Many others from my class have achieved prominence as business people throughout the country.

This era was also the beginnings of the Civil Rights movement. When the sit-ins began at the Woolworth's soda counter in Greensboro, North Carolina, we went to downtown Wilson the very next week and integrated the lunch counters. The first day, we were at the Rose's 5&10; initially, the waitresses just watched us, but made no effort to either remove us or serve us. After about 30 minutes, the manager of the store came over and told them, "Ah hell, just serve them," and just like that, the lunch counter at Rose's was desegregated.

The next day, we went to the Woolworth's store, and the following day, we went to the S. S. Kresge store. We were never sure if the reason desegregation of the lunch counters in Wilson was achieved so peacefully was because of some behind-the-scenes work of our parents or local politicians or because the store managers just decided to do the right thing.

I now know that these were days of struggle for us and our parents, even though I personally felt somewhat sheltered from it all. That feeling of being sheltered and safe was a rarity for most Black folks in Wilson. We could see clearly the disparity between our lives and the lives of our White counterparts. While we did not interact with them, we saw them.

In my early childhood, my dad worked in dry cleaning businesses in Wilson; following his prison stint for bootlegging, he worked at Paramount Cleaners, a White-owned firm in Wilson, and later for Exclusive Cleaners, which was owned by Ed Fulford.

My father's employment with Mr. Fulford is significant because with the assistance of Ed Fulford, my father opened a dry cleaning business of his own in January 1955. I never heard the details of their arrangement, but initially I believe that Ed Fulford was the owner and my dad was the manager. I do recall a discussion between the two of them regarding the fact that my father's title on the window of the cleaners was "Jesse T. Parker, MGR." My father objected to being called manager, and the "MGR" title was removed, but the comma following my dad's name remained on the window for years thereafter.

I don't know when my father became the actual owner of the business, but I do know that he ultimately did own it outright. He operated this business from January 1955 until his death in February 1996, a period of 41 years.

My dad achieved a moderate degree of success with this business and managed to support at least five families in addition to his own as the owner of Friendly Cleaners. While the lifestyle that I had experienced in my very early childhood was never revisited, we were able, for the most part, to live moderately comfortable during these years. As a friend of mine said recently, we were "upper class poor." I worked with my dad in the cleaners until I graduated from high school and left home in 1961.

I have also been reminded by some of my friends of the many times they came to school hungry and that I gave them 25₵ for lunch. Because of my dad's business, I always managed to have at least a few dollars in my pocket. I feel fortunate that I was able to help, but I truly did not remember ever doing it—talk about paying it forward, as this was the same thing that happened to me at Troup Junior High School.

During my childhood, Wilson was an agricultural town. Farmers grew tobacco as their main crop. Tobacco was planted in the spring, harvested in the summer, and sold and processed in the fall. Almost all of this work was done with Black labor. In the spring, the farmers drove their pickup trucks into town in the early mornings and collected the men for the planting season.

This work usually paid about $5 per day. In the summer months, the pay was a bit higher; the White farmers came into town to hire day laborers to harvest the crops. The men were paid about $1 per hour, or $8 per day to work in the fields cropping or harvesting the tobacco. The women were paid $6 per day to either "hand" or tie the tobacco to poles that were used to hang the harvested leaves in barns to be cured for later sale at the warehouses and auction markets in Wilson. At the time, Wilson had the distinction of being known as the "world's largest bright leaf tobacco market".

Some of the Black kids in the area used to make shoe-shine boxes and go to work at the warehouses during the auction season, shining shoes for 10₵ a pair. Others of us used to go the warehouses just to watch the action and feel the excitement.

After the auctions, the processing factories used to start operating and Black people got the jobs at the factories. These operations ran around the clock, every day, until all of the crops had been processed and moved to storage facilities. The typical process at the time was that the factory owners hired large numbers of Black people to work, but allowed them to earn only up to $499 per year because once a person earned $500 in a calendar year, he or she became eligible for unemployment compensation benefits.

Because the minimum wage at the time was only $1 per hour, it was easy to keep most people employed for the entire 8- to 10-week factory season without going over the $499 limit. I worked at a factory on the night shift for about 3 weeks during my senior year in high school. My job was to locate the coded stacks of tobacco that were to be processed by the people on the processing lines and move these stacks to the work areas at the appropriate times. This task usually required 8 hours to complete. On the average night, I'd get the job done in about 3 to 4 hours, and then I'd spend the remainder of the time talking to the ladies on the processing lines. The manager ultimately determined that I was perhaps a bad influence and really not a very good worker and fired me at the end of the third week. It wasn't my kind of work anyway. It was just another sign that I wasn't going to be good at manual labor.

Our high school principal, Mr. Ed Barnes, shared with us at a meeting just prior to our graduation the lengths to which he had gone during his 37-year career to make sure that we did not get a "Negro Education." We got an education that was on a par with or better than any White kid in our town received.

He told us how he never accepted hand-me-down books or used equipment or resources. In the late 1950s, when the White kids got a new high school, he couldn't deliver a completely new school, but we did get a new gymnasium, auditorium, cafeteria, locker rooms, science labs, and classrooms.

Mr. Barnes made sure that the people who taught us were the best teachers available and that they delivered a first-class education. He made sure that all of the kids at our school were prepared for college, even if they couldn't afford to attend. He also made sure that those who weren't going to be attending college were well prepared in the construction trades of brick masonry and carpentry, if that was the direction they wanted to take.

Many of my classmates couldn't afford to attend college, but well over 60% of my fellow graduates did go to college, either immediately or later. I can say unequivocally that Mr. Barnes succeeded in achieving his objectives for the Black children of Wilson, North Carolina.

I have often wondered about the level of benefits that we could have delivered to our home town if we had been allowed to bring our collective resources and intelligence to bear on that place. I think most of us left rather than try.

CHAPTER FOUR

College Years: Shaw University

I attended Shaw University in Raleigh, North Carolina, beginning in September 1961. Shaw was not my first choice for school. I had been accepted to Howard University in Washington, DC, the premier Black university in the nation, and I was prepared to attend. When my father announced that if I didn't attend Shaw University, he wouldn't assist me in any fashion, financially or otherwise, the decision was essentially made *for* me.

I assumed that his reasoning was simply based on family connections. One of my aunts had attended Shaw University in the 1940s. She was the first person in the family to ever attend college. He was determined that I be the second, and to attend the same school.

I later discovered that Shaw University has operated one of the premier boarding schools for

Black children from the eastern North Carolina area and that most of the prominent Black citizens of Wilson had sent their children to Shaw University during the period from 1920 through the 1940s. He probably had in mind that the school still had the same level of prominence as in these earlier times.

My aunt never graduated from Shaw, so I became the first college graduate in the Parker family. Nevertheless I think that Shaw was the only college that my father had ever really heard of and I allowed him to bully me into going; but I really wanted to attend Howard.

Ironically, I was intimidated by the students at Shaw, primarily because, except in very limited cases, these kids had been the valedictorians of their high school classes.

While I had finished in the top five among my classmates, I was comparing them to the caliber of kids with whom I had attended high school.

During freshman talent night, I was encouraged to give an oration, which I had done in high school, on the subject of involvement of the United Nations in the Middle East. I had won second place in a statewide oratory contest during my senior year in high school with this speech.

I was one of the stars of the evening and, on the strength of that speech, I was elected to be president of the freshman class. This office was considered to be a high honor, especially considering that most of the students who nominated and voted for the office were unknown to one another.

When I started college, the Civil Rights movement was in its infancy, but growing quickly. I became an active participant. During this era, I was arrested twice. The first time, I was arrested for attempting to have lunch in the cafeteria of the North Carolina state legislative building. Two colleagues and I went to the cafeteria, entered, and were promptly told that we were not allowed to be there. I insisted that we had a right to be there, primarily because it was a taxpayer-owned and funded facility and my father was a taxpayer in the state of North Carolina.

That argument didn't work too well. Soon after I launched into my explanation, the sergeant at arms of the state senate was summoned and we were arrested and taken to jail in downtown Raleigh, North Carolina. We spent an uncomfortable three days cooling our heels, if not our tempers, in jail. Following this incident, the state legislature quickly passed a new law stating that the cafeteria was only available to serve members of the legislature and their staffs.

Because there were no Black members in the legislature at that time, the place stayed segregated for a while longer. In the interest of full disclosure, I did return to that cafeteria some years later and had lunch. I was not particularly impressed with the food, but at least I was served.

My second arrest in Raleigh came as a result of attempting to enter the S & W cafeteria in downtown Raleigh. I was not jailed for this incident, but I was one of three people charged with assault because I, along with two other colleagues, were trapped in one section of a revolving door with the manager of the restaurant. Although my back was turned to him, we were accused of assaulting him and having caused him bodily harm. No mention was made that he was holding the door to prevent us from entering the restaurant. I was, in fact, convicted of this crime and given a suspended sentence with the provision that I not participate in any further civil rights demonstrations.

As a college freshman, it was difficult for me not to be actively and directly involved in the Civil Rights demonstrations, but cooler heads prevailed and I was convinced by more reasonable people to do my work from the safety of the background.

As students at Shaw University, we conducted marches and protested segregation as much as students in other areas of the country, but without the degree of violence experienced by our contemporaries in places such as Alabama and Mississippi. I have no explanation for this phenomenon. I can only surmise that the leaders of the state of North Carolina were slightly more progressive than other Southern politicians of the day. Remember, if you will, that this was a time when Jesse Helms, who later became a U.S. Senator, was launching his career as a vitriolic right-wing commentator on local television.

I was an active student leader and participated in most aspects of college life. I pledged one of the National Pan- Hellenic Council's historically Black fraternities and sororities, Kappa Alpha Psi fraternity. I became involved in community service activities initiated by the members of my fraternity.

I also participated in various efforts that were put in place by the governor and other political powers in the state designed to appease the Black student population without making significant change to the status quo. It took me a while to recognize that the power structure had no intent of changing very much, if anything.

Nevertheless, I served on a committee established by the governor that was first chaired by Jesse Jackson, who, at the time, was the student body president at North Carolina A&T State University. I became the second chairperson of this committee, which was managed by a young attorney from the governor's staff named John Brooks. John and I became close acquaintances during the course of this activity. During one of our private conversations, he candidly admitted that the purpose of the committee was, basically, to keep us quiet.

At Shaw, I initially chose to major in chemistry, primarily because I had been told that it was important to study the sciences and I had been a fairly good chemistry student in high school. My major changed to history after my sophomore year because I quickly realized that I would never succeed at passing organic chemistry and, to be truthful, I wasn't really interested anyway.

The science professors at Shaw were primarily graduate students from North Carolina State University who seemed more interested in completing their graduate studies and earning a paycheck than in helping and teaching us.

The main focus of Shaw University was to train teachers for elementary and secondary educational careers, and I think they did a good job in this area. However, my primary career goal was always to work in corporate America. Because this time was the beginning of the Civil Rights era, it appeared that opportunities to do so were opening up for Black people—or so I thought. In any event, I never considered doing anything else and I didn't think that I was being unrealistic, as many of my classmates attempted to assure me.

By this time, I had already seen White people succeeding in the corporate world and I was certain that I was at least as smart as they were, if not smarter. I also knew from an early age that life was so much better than anything my classmates and I were experiencing in school. The two things that I was really sure about were that I did not want to be a dry cleaner and I did not want to be a teacher. One of my high school teachers had suggested that I take some education courses so that I would have fallback career; I told her that if I should fall back, it would be on my butt.

I knew the direction that I wanted my life to take and I was not going to let it go for any reason.

CHAPTER FIVE

1963

The year 1963 was an epic one in my life. The summer between my sophomore and junior years of college, my father asked me to stay in Wilson and work with him for the summer. If I did so, he told me, he would pay for me to attend school in the fall.

The previous two summers, I had gone to Atlantic City to work and earned enough money, combined with a scholarship, to pay my own way through school. The scholarship had expired at the end of my sophomore year and I knew that I would be on my own for the next two years.

I really didn't trust my father's promise, but deep in my soul, I really wanted to believe that he would do what he said that he would do. Up until then, he had only contributed about $300 to my education. In spite of my initial trepidation, I stayed and worked at the cleaners that summer. Because I didn't have a regular paycheck, I resorted to taking money from time to time and, on the weekends, I visited my girlfriend Mabel Young, who lived in Raleigh.

I had a checking account at the First Citizens Bank in Raleigh and during these weekend visits, I gave Mabel money to deposit for me at the bank. She did as I asked during the entire summer.

One day in late August, and I still don't know how it happened, my father found my check book. He then demanded that I use the money that I had accumulated, which was about $800, to pay some bills that he had at the cleaners. He assumed correctly that I had pilfered the money, but on the other hand, he had not paid me any salary for working that summer. I had nothing but his promise to pay for school in the fall.

In September, when the time came for me to leave for school, I asked him for the money and he told me that he didn't have it.

This was obviously a very low point in my life; the fear that I had at the beginning of the summer was realized. I had really wanted to believe that he would keep his word, but there was nothing in my history with my father to lead me to think that he would do what he had said that he would do. I think that I just wanted to trust my dad and, for once, not be disappointed by him not keeping his word. His rationale was, of course, that I had stolen from him and therefore didn't deserve anything.

That day was a contentious one for both of us, to the point that by about 6 p.m., I had decided that I was leaving anyway. I was 19 years old and I had $19 in cash in my pocket, which represented the sum total of my worldly assets. I told my father that I was leaving. He was sitting behind the counter at the cleaners and I was standing in the doorway. He asked where I was going and I told him I was going to Raleigh to school. He asked how I intended to do that and I commented that I had no idea but I was indeed leaving. My intent was to take the bus to Raleigh that evening and make whatever arrangements I could.

I turned to walk out of the door and he said to me, "You'll be back soon."

I turned to him and said, "It will be a cold fucking day in hell when you see my black ass again."

I walked out the door with my meager belongings in a small gym bag and headed to the bus station for the 7:30 p.m. bus to Raleigh. I did not see my father again for 9 years. That was clearly another one of my life's defining moments.

The bus ticket cost $3, and the trip took about 1½ hours. I arrived in Raleigh with the remaining $16 and went to 120 South Street, where a friend and I shared a room that cost us $4 per week each for rent. I paid my rent to the landlady early the following morning and was then down to $12 to last me I knew not how long.

The following day, I went to the campus, where most of the kids were registering for classes, I spent most of the day wandering around and wondering what to do. I talked to my girlfriend, Mabel, who was upset that I didn't have the money because she knew that I had been saving during the summer. She thought the funds were available. Needless to say, that was a rather miserable day for me and for her on my behalf.

At the end of that day, I walked to downtown Raleigh, for no particular purpose other than to think. During that stroll, I passed the Air Force recruitment office where two men were working. I walked a past a few yards, then turned around, and walked in.

I talked with the recruiters about joining the Air Force. I told them that my preference was to fly if I joined. They said that being a pilot required a college degree. Because I didn't have one, I could go in as a navigator because I had completed two years of college. Being a navigator would allow me to achieve my goal of flying.

They arranged for me to leave that same evening for Seymour Johnson Air Force Base in Goldsboro, North Carolina, to take the aviation cadet's exam, scheduled for the following morning. I was given a travel voucher for the bus trip, and a $25 voucher for expenses and incidentals, plus instructions to appear at the bachelor officers' quarters for housing that night.

The following morning, I awoke, put myself together, and went to the testing site.

Approximately 25 people were already there, preparing themselves to take the exam. I listened carefully to the monitor's instructions. After reviewing the exam, I was convinced that I knew the answers to each question; they were really easy. Because I knew all 100 answers, I finished early and proceeded to review my answers.

After the first part of the exam, we were excused for lunch. When we returned from lunch, I was advised by the monitor that I had failed the exam. To my surprise, I didn't have any correct answers; in fact, my answers were 100 percent incorrect. I didn't believe him because I really knew all of the answers to the questions on the exam, and I was positive that my answers were correct. He assured me that I had not answered any of the questions correctly. I was dismissed.

Strangely enough, I was not upset and really took the news as a sign that I was not supposed to go into the Air Force. The next day, I returned to Raleigh and reported my failure to the Air Force recruiters, who already knew the results. They tried to get me to enlist anyway but I declined, choosing instead to return to school.

Mabel asked what I planned to do. By midday, though, I had an idea. I visited Shaw's business manager, Thomas Kee. I laid out a plan: get a job and attend school part-time (12 credit hours/3 classes) and pay semester tuition at $20/week until it was all paid. Mr. Kee agreed to this arrangement and my third year of college began.

The next day I got a job as busboy and waiter at the S & W Cafeteria in downtown Raleigh. The salary was the $20/week I needed to pay the school, plus a meal per day and it allowed me to earn tips, which I hoped would meet other needs. It seemed ironic that I got a job at the same establishment where I'd been arrested just two years earlier. It was also here that I discovered that I was not destined for a career in food service.

My first day on the job, the supervisor showed me where the lockers were. He told me to change into the necessary uniform. He detailed how to provide appropriate service to customers. Most importantly, it seemed, were instructions on use of the employees' dining area, where employees were to take any meals they ate at the restaurant.

I took in all of his instructions, donned a uniform, and started work that very day on the lunch shift. Work went smoothly. I think I adequately kept the tables cleaned and carried patrons' trays to their table as they exited the cafeteria lines.

At the end of the lunch-time rush, I noticed most of the employees leaving the floor to go to their own lunch. Now, while the supervisor had shown me the employees' dining area, he had not provided the most important detail: where to get the food to be eaten in the employees' dining area.

I noticed the maintenance man (a White person) was getting his lunch. He picked up a tray and went down the back side of the cafeteria line and the serving ladies gave him what he requested. Assumed this was the procedure, I did the same. The ladies served me, just as they had the maintenance man, and I took my tray downstairs to the employee dining area, the same one the supervisor had told me about earlier that same day.

Reaching the dining area, I discovered the news of my having picked up my meal had preceded me. The other employees were laughing and talking about it. Naturally, I thought this was a little strange because I assumed that everyone got their food the same way. I had not been told that the food for Black people was prepared downstairs in a small kitchen adjoining the employee dining area.

By the time I took my seat, the supervisor was coming for me. Before I could take a bite, he began berating me for thinking that I was better than everyone else. I was confused. I didn't understand what he was talking about—food was food. I was eating where he told me to eat, but he then pointed out that I thought I was better than the other Black people because I got my food upstairs.

Having satisfied himself that I was both completely humiliated and utterly chastised, he took my tray and dumped the food into the garbage. He pointed toward the door and told me to get out. That was the end of my short-lived career at the S & W Cafeteria.

Despite the loss of yet another source of income, I managed to stay in school on the terms that I negotiated. When I returned to Mr. Kee and explained the loss of my job, he arranged for me to become the sports reporter for the school's athletic teams. At the time, the mainstream media did not cover Black collegiate sports. This job paid $20 per week, which covered my weekly debt to the school.

I still needed money for food, rent, and incidentals. I'm not sure how I managed, but, by the grace of God, with the help of some very good friends, I made it through that period.

At the beginning of the second semester of that school year, Mr. Kee told me the National Defense Student Loans Program. I became one of the first loan recipients at our school, allowing me to complete my college education. I borrowed a total of $1,200.

My college experience was interesting in many respects, but disappointing in others.

The educational aspect was a particular letdown. I was left with the feeling that my high school education was much better than my college education, and did a much better job of preparing me for life and living in the real world.

One of the brightest spots of my college life was being elected as freshman class president after that oration on freshman talent night. That and my job as sports reporter ultimately led to my being selected as editor of the student newspaper and of the 1965 yearbook.

In 1963 and 1964 I was elected to lead our school's delegation to the statewide Model United Nations Conferences held annually, usually at the University of North Carolina at Chapel Hill or Duke University. I was also elected in 1964 as the delegation leader of our legislative team, which met with others from colleges across the state for the annual mock legislative session. We met for five days at the old state house in Raleigh.

These experiences were not specifically designed for Black students. In fact, only three of North Carolina's 13 Black colleges then participated in these events. These programs were to teach White students how the legislative process worked and to provide experience in governance and politics at the state and international levels. I still managed to take full advantage of these opportunities and often inserted myself into the midst of the deliberations and debates on most of the issues addressed by the mock assemblies. Because of my audacity—my innate not "knowing my place"— positioning myself in the middle of things, I gained a reputation around the state for my outspokenness.

These experiences also gave me my first independent exposure to racism on a personal level. I remember one event in particular. A group of us—Blacks and Whites together—who were in the mock legislative assembly were turned away from a restaurant in downtown Raleigh because the owner didn't allow Black people in his establishment. The White kids who were part of our group refused to enter the establishment when the owner wouldn't let us Blacks enter.

On another occasion, the student legislative delegations were invited to a fraternity party at North Carolina State College. Several of us went, thinking that it was a legitimate invitation. We were quickly disabused of the notion that the invitation extended to Black students.

Not feeling entirely comfortable with the environment, we had a few drinks; there seemed to be a concerted effort by our hosts to ostracize us. As soon as we were outside the door, the music started playing. I guess they intended that little jab to be an insult, but we just laughed at the stupidity of it all and wondered why they had bothered to invite us in the first place.

Prior to my college years, I had essentially been sheltered from the direct scourge of racism. Of course, I knew that racism existed, after all I had been arrested for attempting to desegregate a cafeteria at the state legislative building, but I felt my life was apart from it. I couldn't relate to other people's stories because they were so very different from mine. Besides, I don't think I ever genuinely cared. I was focused on where I wanted to go and I was certain that nothing as silly as another person's racist behavior was going to stop me.

CHAPTER SIX

Washington, DC, and the 1965 Inaugural Committee

In November 1964, I was a student intern with the 1965 Presidential Inaugural Committee in Washington, DC. The opportunity to participate, however distantly, with Lyndon Johnson and Hubert Humphrey came courtesy of that guardian angel, Thomas Kee of Shaw University. The assignment was to be with the Young Democrats of America. I was roommates with Franklin "Frank" Delano Rozak from Detroit. Frank was a Young Democrats national leader and, through him, I was able to meet a number of Washington and national political dignitaries, including J. Albert House of North Carolina, the national president of the Young Democrats.

Despite the fact that the plan for the three-month internship was to be with the Young

Democrats of America, Frank told me that Al House was not going to allow that opportunity to be given to a Black kid. Instead, I ended up working in the general office supply area. Being a supply clerk wasn't much of a job, but the overall experience was outstanding.

Despite being relegated to office supplies, I enjoyed the status of a Washington dignitary. I was one of the very few paid civilian staffers on the inaugural committee, and that position carried a special status all its own. More than 90 percent of the staff were volunteers or military personnel.

I was a complete novice in this situation. I absolutely did not understand that the main reason for volunteering in Washington was to gain access to people through whom one could get a government job. Almost all of the people with whom I interacted daily were trying to get a government job in the new Johnson Administration.

I quickly came to understand that most White people, as opposed to most Black people that I know, are completely ruthless when it comes to matters of gaining influence and advantage in all situations involving prestige or money. I also realized that they didn't consider Black people to represent any threat to their hegemony, primarily because they never came into contact with any Black people and had no frame of reference. Only one other Black person was actually paid for working on the 1965 Inaugural Committee. She was a women in the public relations office.

My experience working for the Inaugural Committee was one of those times when a mentor would have been really helpful. I think having a mentor in that situation would have changed the entire direction of my life. I have sometimes wondered whether I would have been able to get a mentor if I had not been Black.

In any event, I think I made the best of the situation. I participated at the highest levels in the inauguration of Johnson and Humphrey. I attended the Young Democrats of America's Inaugural Ball. I could invite many of my friends and acquaintances to the inaugural festivities.

The one invitation that I missed sending, and to this day I truly regret, was to Dr. Carl DeVane, my political science professor at Shaw University. I learned upon my return to school that he had desperately wanted an invitation, but he never asked and no one told me — until it was too late. I still remember this unintentional slight on my part. I'm sure that one reason that I always try to speak up for others is that this inadvertent oversight had such a profound impact on me. I missed the opportunity to make a kind gesture—such a simple task—toward a person who was important to me and was instrumental in making me the person I became.

I think my efforts to make the most of my experience on the Inaugural Committee were at least somewhat successful. I never really aspired to a career in politics or government service, but I should have done more to maintain some of those relationships. Unfortunately, I never saw any of those people again after the celebrations ended.

At the end of the three months, in February 1965, I returned to school to start preparing for June graduation. Soon, I would seek my fame and fortune in the real world.

During the senior recruitment season, I had two job interviews. The first was with Eastern Airlines as a customer service representative. I couldn't believe Eastern Airlines was seriously recruiting college graduates for such a job, but I was assured the opportunity was completely legitimate. This was 1965, and the corporate job market was opening up to Black People, legitimate job or not, I wasn't remotely interested in working in the customer service department for an airline or anyone else. I had my sights set exclusively on the higher rungs of the corporate ladder.

My second interview was with two recruiters from the U.S. State Department for a position in the Foreign Service. I admit that this opportunity did have some appeal because of the glamour of foreign travel. Thankfully, I did not get a job offer.

If I had, I probably would have become a government bureaucrat.

The State Department interviewers introduced me to *The Man*, by Irving Wallace. It tells the story of a man who, through a series of unlikely events, became the first Black president of the United States.

After reading *The Man*, I joined the Book of the Month Club and remained a loyal member for about 25 years. Thus, I was among the first to learn of new books.

I had been introduced to books as a young child visiting the small public library in Wilson. *The Man* returned me to daily reading. I remain a voracious reader of all sorts of books, but my favorites are biographies.

My remaining months in college were memorable primarily because what happened at the end. Three days before graduation, I was summoned to the president's office for a 7:30 a.m. meeting. Upon arrival, I came face to face with the members of the university council: the deans and department heads of each area of the university, and the administrative heads of the school. It appeared that I had committed the most egregious of infractions—I had omitted a senior's photograph from the yearbook. Now, this mistake was not my direct doing, but as editor of the yearbook, I was responsible. In fact, it turned out that *two* seniors' photographs had been omitted.

Most of the yearbook work had been done while I was in Washington, doing my internship with the Inaugural Committee. That excuse didn't fly with the university council members. I was the editor and I was responsible. To this day, I believe an alternative agenda was at work: the members of the council believed I had violated the unwritten rule about not making business decisions related to student affairs without the administration's approval. No one explicitly stated that I had violated the secret code, but I sensed it nonetheless.

My mistake was serious to those on the university council, and the list they gave me detailing my punishment was a lengthy one: immediate expulsion from the university, a permanent letter of reprimand entered into my record, and award of my degree one year later and in *absentia*. In addition, I was required to reimburse the two individuals for the money they had spent for the yearbook and apologize to the senior class for my transgressions.

Further, I was not to discuss or reveal this punishment to anyone. I felt this was a stupid requirement because I had to tell someone if I was to apologize. Shaw's president at the time was James Cheek, who later became president of Howard University in Washington, DC.

I reached an all-time low point of my life on that morning. All of my struggles to get to that point were immediately rendered useless. I felt as though I had wasted 4 years and I was being catapulted into the world alone, without a diploma, and I had absolutely no idea where to turn for help.

There was no clear way out of the dilemma. Graduation for everyone else in my class was only two days away. Alumni and families were gathering for the weekend; baccalaureate services were scheduled for Sunday; the family graduation dinner was to be held on Saturday evening; and the commencement exercises were set for Monday.

Lenoir Cook, dean of the undergraduate college, called a senior class meeting for three o'clock that afternoon. The nature of the meeting was not announced publicly, but I was the main attraction. The sole purpose of the meeting was to provide a forum for my apology.

I felt shell-shocked. As I sat outside the student union building, looking forlorn and lost, Elizabeth Cofield, a Shaw professor, approached. I had never taken any of her classes, but she had always taken an interest in me, I think because of my activism. I don't remember many specifics of this encounter but I related the morning's events in the president's office.

She called the two students whose photos had been unintentionally omitted from the yearbook. They and I got together to discuss the situation. While we all recognized the seriousness of leaving a senior's photo out of the yearbook — much less two seniors' photos —none of us agreed with the harshness of the punishment that was handed down. One person was satisfied with having her money returned ($7.50) and the other person didn't want the money. I gave it to him anyway, and offered personal apologies to each of them. I spent most of the next few hours thinking about what I was going to say to the senior class members who had been instructed to assemble at 3 p.m. to hear my apology.

My speech was not very long, but I do believe that I was guided by the hand of God to say what I did.

Before I began my apology, I remembered a conversation of perhaps a year or so earlier with John Brooks. John was the governor's liaison to the Black student community in North Carolina. His role in the governor's administration was to develop an outreach project to the Black schools.

John and I collaborated on the unwinnable task of working on a "keep busy" project which was to research and publish a series of pamphlets on the *Black contributions to the development of North Carolina*. One day, as we were traveling to somewhere, we discussed our respective schools. He was a recent graduate of the University of North Carolina at Chapel Hill—both undergraduate and law school. He recounted how at UNC, the president of the student council sat on the school's advisory board and represented the students' viewpoint to the administration. This notion fascinated me; at Shaw University, students had no option to participate in any area of the school's operations, nor did students have any input into what went on at the school relative to their education or welfare.

As our conversation continued, John told me how the students at UNC were taught and allowed to run all issues of student affairs at the school—the newspaper, student publications, housing, and so on. John was amazed that students everywhere didn't have the same level of involvement and authority. Mind you, he attended a predominately White university and I was attending—until my expulsion—an HBCU.

College is supposed to be about teaching students how to master adult responsibilities and to maneuver through the world beyond college. I remember explaining my belief about this type of instruction being the real reason that people attended school: to be trained in how to "be" in the world and to think independently and interact in real-life situations.

As I pondered my apology to the senior class, it dawned on me that, after four years of so-called training, none of my fellow Shaw University students had any inkling of how to navigate successfully in the world beyond getting a job teaching—and I knew that teaching was not my destiny.

I carried that frame of mind into the lecture hall that afternoon. My address to the senior class began with a recap of my conversation with John Brooks. I reminded my classmates that I had indeed made a grievous error that had caused two people distress.

The mistake was neither intentional nor life-threatening, but it was a mistake and, as editor of the yearbook, I was ultimately responsible for what anyone on the yearbook staff had done. I was there to apologize publicly for what amounted to someone else's error.

Rather than throw myself on my sword, as the members of the university council had expected, I posed a question to my classmates: "Why we are not allowed to make mistakes at this institution? We are students, and the purpose of school is to teach and train students. If we are not allowed to make a mistake here, then how are we supposed to learn?"

"If we don't know how to conduct business and we are not allowed to manage and conduct the business that involves us here, then how can we be expected to conduct business when we leave this place to go into the wider world?"

"What is the purpose of school, if not to teach and train students? I made some mistakes, and it appears that some of them involved making business decisions with which the administration of the school did not agree."

"I decided to do business with vendors who were not selected by the administrators, but I was given no direction in advance about vendors with whom I should and should not do business; after the fact, I am to be punished for taking the initiative and making a decision that went against protocol or someone else's hidden agenda."

"I was instructed to not discuss the matter of my punishment, but I think you need to know the conclusions reached by the administration. The punishment is severe and includes my not being able to graduate with you, my classmates, on Monday. The reason I was given for this punishment is that I left the photographs of two classmates out of the yearbook. This did indeed happen, but it was not intentional, and I personally apologized to the wronged students and I now publicly apologize to all of you."

After I finished my speech, Jacqueline Edmunds, a classmate from Camden, New Jersey, rose to address Dean Cook and the class.

"Dean Cook," said Jacqueline, "if Parker doesn't march with us on Monday, you can cancel the graduation because none of us will march."

"Ain't that right, class?" she added for good measure.

She got an overwhelming ovation and everyone agreed the graduation would not be held—or that at least no graduating seniors would participate—if I couldn't participate.

Later that day, I was again summoned to the president's office and all of the previous sanctions were deemed null and void because I had agreed to repay the two individuals the money that they had spent for their yearbooks. No apology was offered to me for the shame they had intended to inflict. I have only returned to Shaw University once during the ensuing years, on the 10th anniversary of my graduation.

CHAPTER SEVEN

Graduation and New York City

I got married while I was still in college to Alice Mitchell. Alice was five years older than I, but our relationship, which started during my freshman year, had endured through much of my first semester on campus. We broke up during the second semester because a fellow who she had dated for the prior three years returned to get his teaching credentials, and they resumed their relationship.

Alice was the first person since I'd left Wilson to say I was "different." She told me one day, shortly after I arrived on campus, that she used to observe the young men who were standing "on the block" by the student union. It was a typical gathering spot for students following meals and or classes. Right away, she noticed that I was different from all the other guys. She made it a point to meet me and start a relationship.

Alice graduated at the end of my freshman year and I did not hear from her again until early 1964. I received a letter she sent via a mutual friend. She was working in New York City and wanted to rekindle our relationship.

Her letter reached me at an especially difficult time. I'd just finished the first semester of my junior year, the year in which I had only the $20 per week for tuition and no money for much of anything else. I survived with the help of some wonderful friends. My father had reneged on his promise to pay for college, perhaps to get me back to Wilson and the dry cleaning business, but I was adamantly not doing that.

Soon after Alice reached out, she made it clear that she wanted to get married. I was desperate for money. She later admitted that she was desperate to free herself from her father's demands for $150 per month as repayment for his funding her college education

With our eyes wide open, Alice and I entered an unholy alliance based entirely on our mutual needs. Alice had told me years earlier that she knew that I was different; she believed that I would be successful. She intended to attach herself to that success. We married.

Upon graduation, I went to New York City, because my wife was there, and my future in corporate America beckoned more brightly in that environment than in any other that I knew.

I immediately started my career search, without any guidance or coaching. I had never had a real job, and I really didn't have much of an idea about how to find one.

I began by reading the help wanted ads. I was especially looking for companies advertising for management and sales positions. My first job offer came rather quickly from the retailer E. J. Korvette as a stock clerk. I thought to myself, "*No, thanks.*" I quickly began to understand why Eastern Airlines thought that a customer service representatives job was a good offer—it was certainly at least one rung higher up the ladder than stock clerk!.

I later answered an ad posted by the Singer Sewing Machine Company for a sales representative position. I responded and went for an interview. I was administered their standard entry-level test—the Wonderlic® test. I think I was supposed to be eliminated by this test, but I scored 100 percent.

I overheard someone say that mine was the highest test score ever recorded by anyone in the company. They weren't sure what to do with me, so they had me wait in a conference room while a series of people passed by the door to look in at me.

After waiting for almost an hour, a fellow who appeared to be in charge came in from lunch. He was approached by a number of staffers, who apprised him of the situation, that situation being me—a Black man—and my all-time-high score. He then came into the conference room and promptly told me there were no openings and that I should leave immediately. End of discussion. I didn't even get to ask any questions about the validity of the advertisement in the newspaper, which I still had with me. Clearly, I was hopelessly naïve. It didn't occur to me until later what had happened. After reflecting on the situation for a few days, I realized that I had been the victim of racial discrimination.

After several other attempts at finding suitable employment, I responded to an advertisement for a new employment agency, Richard Clarke and Associates. I was probably among its first clients. This agency went on to become one of the best known and most effective employment agencies for Black executives in the nation.

I signed up when it was a one-man operation. Richard worked in a small office with a stack of files on his cluttered desk. Despite the somewhat less than impressive surroundings, this encounter worked for me. Richard Clarke referred me to Union Carbide Corporation for a sales representative position, thus starting me on my journey through White corporate America.

My initial encounter with Union Carbide was interesting, to put it mildly. I arrived at the human resources department during lunch and had to wait until the person I was there to see returned. While waiting, another fellow, a White man, came in to meet with that same person. When he returned, he called in the White guy first. My heart promptly sank. However, after only a few minutes, the White guy was escorted out and I was invited in.

It just so happened that the interviewer was a Black man, but he was very light skinned and I didn't recognize him as a Black man initially. He apologized and indicated that he was aware that I had arrived first, but he knew that he would make short work of the interview with the other fellow and didn't want anything to interfere with the time that I needed.

He shared with me that he had been the second Black professional ever hired by that company and that, hopefully, I would be the third. I wish I could remember his name, but I can't. Three months after I was hired, he left Union Carbide.

I was referred to the consumer products division, the division responsible for Prestone® antifreeze and Eveready® batteries. The day following my human resources interview, I had 18 interviews with the management of that division. I literally talked to everyone who was in the office that day.

After a full morning of interviews, I was invited to lunch. Before we were to leave, I went to the restroom, but when I returned, everyone was gone. I looked throughout the office and could find no one at all—not even a secretary who could tell me where everyone else had gone! It was as if they had all disappeared, so I went to lunch by myself. When I returned from lunch, everyone was asking what happened to me, as if *I* had been the one to disappear from the group. It was strange, but I said, "I had just gone to the restroom and, when I came out, I noticed everybody had gone." I never got an explanation. That afternoon, the interview process continued.

The final interview that day was with C. J. "Jack" Van Winkle, president of the division, who offered me $500 per month to start as a sales representative. I found out later that the offer was a low-ball, $200 below the market rate and the salaries being offered to my White counterparts at the time. I was happy to get the offer because at least I had achieved my objective, which was to work in corporate America and to make at least $500 a month.

Because I had no role models or experienced people to give me guidance about the salary, and my $500 a month salary represented the highest paying job that a Shaw University graduate had managed to get up to that time, I was sure I had a firm hold on the brass ring. Shaw University was a school primarily committed to training Black Teachers, several of whom had graduated at the same time as I did, and had taken jobs in Las Vegas. The going rate for teachers at that time was about \$4,800/year (equivalent to \$27,400 today), an unheard of salary for Black teachers in the mid-1960s. Given this situation my point of reference was rather low because my goal was to make at least \$6,000/year (equivalent to \$34,200 today) but I was comparing apples to turnips.

I should have been paid \$8,400/year (equivalent to \$47,900 today) because that was the starting salary offered to all new hires, except all the new hires—but me—were White. Because of my inexperience, ignorance about the salary structure, and minimal negotiating skills I was basically cheated out of the equivalent of \$13,000 in annual salary. And I still had to pay a finder's fee to the employment agency.

A troubling aspect of this employment equation which allows people to be underpaid is that it still exists in America. It is manifested in the secrecy surrounding salaries. I believe this practice allows people of all stripes to be underpaid and unfairly devalued. I am often puzzled by the thinking of people who decide to pay a person less money than another person to do a job based solely on the color of the person's skin or, in the case of women, the person's gender. No matter how hard

I try to make sense of this situation, I just can't wrap my mind around the "logic" of it.

So there I was, the third Black professional hired by Union Carbide, one of three among 103,000 employees. The first Black professional employee was Albert Stewart, an organic chemist with a doctorate who was hired in 1948 at the Oak Ridge Tennessee Nuclear Facility which was managed by Union Carbide. Dr. Stewart told me that all of the employees of that facility, including the maintenance staff voted as to whether he would be hired, obviously he won the election.

I had been hired as a salesperson, but I was never allowed to go into the field as a salesman.

My initial assignment was in the Northeast sales office in New York City as an inside account representative. I was told this position was a training assignment, designed for me to gain product knowledge before a field assignment, first with the Prestone® car care line and then with Eveready® batteries. I was never told specifically what the job duties entailed. I guessed I was supposed to watch the other people in the office and figure it out.

After six months in the Northeast sales office, I was transferred to the operations area of the division headquarters. I was to replace Bob Goldie, who was retiring. To this day, I am not sure what Bob's job was, but when I arrived at his office, I encountered a desk that was covered with a stack of papers two feet deep across every available surface, including his credenza. Bob was tasked to train me for his job during his last two weeks.

I don't think that he had any idea about what he was doing, and if he did, he didn't see fit to impart any of that knowledge to me. Once again, I found myself in a YOYO ("You're On Your Own") job situation.

After a week of Bob's "training," I decided to stay late one night and I swept the desk clean. I threw every scrap of paper into the trash.

The following morning, he arrived to a clean desk, probably for the first time since the beginning of his career. He asked me if I had seen a particular item that he had been working on from the prior day, and I said I had not. At the end the day, he left permanently.

I still had not been given a job description or a list of duties. I guess people assumed that I would just know what to do. So I created a job based largely on the requests from the people who called and who had previously dealt with Bob.

Ultimately, I became the person responsible for purchasing the automobile fleet for the sales force, as well as for selecting and contracting with vendors for promotional premiums used for sales contests and customer incentives. I arranged purchases of tickets to Broadway shows and other special events for important customers and executives. Eventually, my job became one that required me to function as a fleet buyer, premium incentive buyer, and corporate concierge. I'm not sure if this is what Bob did because neither he nor anyone else told me what Bob's role had been.

The job had a lot of perks and benefits, most of them provided by the vendors of the various items that I purchased and for which I arranged contracts.

I was usually invited to join my co-workers for drinks after work. For some Union Carbide employees, the after-work drinks started at lunch. Most of them headed home to the suburbs after a few drinks in the evening; I headed for our apartment in the Bedford-Stuyvesant area of Brooklyn.

The most difficult part of working for Union Carbide was what I perceived to be an almost total disregard for people in general and what I considered to be a lack of respect for me as a person specifically.

Management didn't seem to have a clue about what I was doing. Perhaps the contract sizes were insignificant. At that time, Union Carbide was such a large and profitable organization that the dollars spent on things in the area of my purview seemed to be relatively meaningless. In time, management's arrogance would prove be very costly.

It took me only a little time to realize that most of my White colleagues were essentially in the same position as I was—stuck in jobs that they didn't like or appreciate. They were doing work that they didn't consider particularly useful, relevant or challenging, and they appeared to be going through the motions to be seen as relevant and worthy.

My initial foray into corporate America was not turning out as I had envisioned. It wasn't a place of creative energy and efficiency where talented people collaborated for the good of the company and society. Instead, corporate America appeared to be a place where White men went to construct elaborate charades of success and to perpetuate the myth of invincibility behind which they hid their insecurities. Even so, I was not prepared to abandon my dream nor my objective, which was still to rise to the top of a major American corporation.

Dr. Stewart, the organic chemist and the only other Black man at the corporate headquarters, convinced me to stay at Union Carbide for at least two years. Staying in a job I didn't enjoy and working for a company whose management I didn't respect was a tremendous chore, but I stuck it out. He had promised to help me look for another job if I stayed for at least that long, and he kept his word. I did get some offers from his efforts mostly from nonprofit organizations, I had also begun searching on my own.

I landed a job with Manufacturers Hanover Bank, but I quickly rejected it. I made my decision after I had reviewed the bank's training manual, which detailed very specifically each task to be done hour-by-hour over a 3-year training period. This level of micromanagement would have driven me nuts. My natural tendency is decidedly averse to mind-numbing detail. In retrospect, that training regimen would have probably been good for me to undergo, considering that I had no training whatsoever in any position that I had held since the S & W Cafeteria.

Another reason I declined the job at Manufacturers Hanover was pressure from an employment agency recruiter. Later, I discovered that he didn't want me to take the job so he could make a commission from a different company. He referred me to the INA Insurance Company, where I was actually offered a job starting in the mailroom. The individual who extended this offer wore such a look of self-satisfaction that I just couldn't accept the job. He seemed to believe that his offer was going to make such a difference in my life that I couldn't possibly refuse it. I was not impressed with the offer and immediately turned it down. The employment agency recruiter went totally ballistic because I didn't accept the "great job" he had found for me. So much for ethics in the workplace.

Undaunted, I pursued other opportunities at West Virginia Pulp and Paper Company and the J. Walter Thompson Advertising Agency. The people with whom I met were minimally courteous, but no job offers were extended.

During August 1967, I attended a job fair and met Harold Bass, a recruiter from Eastman Kodak Company. He made me an offer contingent upon moving to Rochester, New York. I accepted, much to the chagrin of my wife, Alice, who did not want to leave New York City.

CHAPTER EIGHT

Eastman Kodak Company

I was to start at Kodak in September 1967, but we ran into a problem on our initial visit to Rochester, New York in order to find housing. We visited the Kodak home office and the Human Resources Department where we were introduced to three Black employees -- Jim Hines, Hollis Holland and Dick Ricketts, a former professional basketball player.

They shared information about the community and available apartments. Jim Hines suggested the apartment complex where he and his family lived. We called the rental office and we were told that they had lots of units available and that all we needed to do was to come in and sign a lease. Alice was pregnant with our first child, Gregory, and was not planning to work, so this place seemed perfect because it was close to my new office. Jim assured us that the place was very nice, and that we would be pleased with the facilities and the location.

When we arrived at the rental office, the resident manager told us that there were no apartments available. We protested this claim and indicated that we had called and were told a lot of units were available. I knew we were being discriminated against but I couldn't understand why because the Hines family already lived there.

In any event, we went back to the Kodak Human Resources office and called again. We were told again that they had many vacancies. I recognized the voice as that of the same person who denied us an apartment in person.

We went back and confronted him and he reluctantly agreed to lease us a place but said that it would not be available for 30 days. Because Alice was pregnant, she really didn't want to fight and argue, so I relented and we agreed to move to Rochester one month later. Thinking back on it, I really was disappointed that the human resources personnel at Kodak did not take any action on our behalf. I guess this was simply a harbinger of things to come.

During the month I had to wait for the apartment in Rochester, I did some work as an employment counselor for the employment agency that had sent me to the insurance company mail room. This was also my first experience working in an environment with all Jewish People. Here I discovered that these folks routinely changed their given names to "professional" Christian-sounding names for work purposes.

We moved to Rochester on October 1, 1967. We settled into the Rochester community quite well and made friends easily. Kodak was on a hiring binge during that period and brought in many Black employees across the company. As in most organizations of that size, however, they were able to keep most of us isolated from each other by assigning us to widely separated departments.

We became friendly with the Hines family because, like us, they were a young couple and had one child, a son named Alvin. Jim, we also discovered, was a former employee of Union Carbide. He was an industrial engineer professionally and had worked for Union Carbide at their battery plant in Greenville, North Carolina. His stint at Union Carbide had begun shortly after they had hired me in New York City.

Jim was a native of Greenville, a town located only 37 miles from Wilson. So we felt that we had a lot in common even though we had never known of each other prior to our meeting in Rochester.

My Kodak experience lasted 10 years. I started in the Distribution Systems Development Group. At the time, this was a primary entry level place for new hires. Six people were in my class, and soon after starting work, I again discovered that my salary was less than my White counterparts'. I was being paid $700 per month and everyone else was earning $800 per month.

I was now two years out of college and my pay had only increased by $200 a month. This was a situation that plagued my entire career at Kodak. I was chronically underpaid during all of the years that I worked at the company.

Kodak's plan for new hires in the Distribution Systems Development Group was to train them in the company's logistics and warehousing processes and allow them to develop new systems and procedures to be used throughout the company's vast distribution network, both domestically and internationally.

These networks were large and geographically diverse. New employees to this arena were considered to be the future managers of the company. Most Kodak managers were promoted to district offices after a stint in this division, so I finally felt that I had arrived at the place of which I had dreamed. I had completed a number of very interesting assignments in the US and abroad, including stints in Puerto Rico, Brazil and Venezuela. These assignments mostly involved analyzing and evaluating warehousing, logistics systems and product handling procedures. My job was to design ways to make these systems and procedures more efficient and effective.

My international experience was interesting and productive. I received high praise from most of the field managers that I worked with and thought these assignments would have prepared me for work in Kodak's international division, but, as I later discovered, this was not going to happen.

In the third year of my tenure, my immediate supervisor, Ed Steck, asked me to join him in a new assignment in Kodak's main distribution center. I was to be Ed's assistant at this two million square foot, state of the art, warehouse and shipping facility in Rochester. What I didn't realize was that Ed was being relegated to "purgatory" and he wanted company.

I don't know the circumstances, but Ed had become *persona non grata*. It took me a year to escape this situation at which time I assumed a low level supervisory position in the advertising distribution area. In order to create this positon for me management moved a 25 year White employee aside temporarily. When I left the position he resumed his old job.

After a year in this supervisory positon, I had reached the magical five-year point. Every other member of my induction class had been promoted to a district manager's job; I was the only one left.

Then the skies opened for me — a new district manager's position opened in Seattle, Washington.

I started preparing for the move. We began getting the Seattle newspapers to look for housing and to get a feel for the community. After almost two weeks of hearing nothing, I was summoned to the human resources office to discuss my future with the company.

I practically floated to the meeting at the appointed time, fully expecting to be told that we were being relocated to Seattle. My swollen head was soon severely deflated. Rather than Seattle, I was asked to relocate to Washington, DC. I considered this carefully and thought that this would be OK, particularly given the state of affairs in the country and in the company at the time. Plus, Washington, DC was touted to be a "Black City." Therefore, I felt OK with the offer until I asked where the current manager of the Washington office was going. I was told that he wasn't going anywhere and that I would be expected to work for him as his customer service manager (there was that customer service job again).

I'd shared a cubicle with this guy for three years as a peer. While we had a good cordial relationship, I was totally unprepared for this scenario.

I declined the job. I was also told that if I didn't accept that position, they had no idea what they could do for me. I asked if I was being fired and they said that I wasn't but, if I wanted to leave, it was up to me. I elected to keep the position in Advertising Distribution for a while longer.

About six months later, I had lunch with Bill Irons, my manager. We were discussing my situation and the Seattle job. He told me that everyone in management in the division knew that I was designated for the Seattle job. He told me I didn't get the job because the regional manager for the Pacific region, said that he wouldn't have any "niggers working for him." With the assistance of Bill Irons, I managed to move from the distribution division into the consumer products division and into sales promotion. This was not a smooth transition. In this case my new supervisor and coworkers knew I was being placed on hold and they were reluctant to have me working with them. It was truly an "Old Boys Club" environment.

I was the only person in the sales promotion office other than the manager who had not previously been in the field as a sales rep. And this job represented a significant promotion for these people. I was encouraged many times to go into the field as a sales representative, but I refused because I was never given any assurance about where I'd be assigned or if I'd be able to advance from the position. Given my prior experiences with Kodak, I was not willing to take the chance. My tenure in the sales promotion area was at least interesting. The people there really didn't have a job for me, but I managed to carve out a niche which I think surprised and, in some fashion, shocked most of them.

I was in my sixth year at Kodak when I started this job and I asked many times what my job was supposed to be. The answer was always, "Your job is what you make it." I think I was probably the last person that they ever made that statement to. Because over the course of the next four years, I turned that position into the *defacto* Head of Sales Promotions for Kodak film in the United States and Canada. I believe that my audaciousness in assuming that position really pissed off a lot of people. This became more apparent near the end of my tenure with the company, during my final year at Kodak the Consumer Products Division President would call regularly to inquire as to the state of my "busyness"

He always wanted to know if I was busy, and more specifically, what I was working on. His questioning initially annoyed me, so one day I told him that I felt a more important question would be, "Am I effective, not just busy?" He realized that I was irritated so he shared his reasoning for asking the question so frequently, which was that film was such an important part of the product mix, and at the time, it accounted for over $4 billion of sales. He wanted to know what I was doing so consistently because my level of activity gave him good insight into the status of sales and promotional activity in the marketplace.

I encountered him in Atlanta long after he retired, and he told me that he had been very frustrated with the people at Kodak because, for the most part, they were, "...stupid, inflexible and totally unwilling to look at new ideas and concepts."

Life in Rochester was good in a strange way. I had a job which I really enjoyed doing at the end of my tenure, but it was not financially rewarding.

I associated primarily with White people, at work, as there were very few Black folk in the division.

However, during this time we moved into the upper middle class of Rochester's "Black Society." I became a board member of local Urban League; as a result, I became one of the "leaders of the community." I along with several other people would meet, periodically, with the real movers and shakers of the Rochester community, namely the CEO's of the major companies and leading local institutions.

On several occasions, I had breakfast with Walter Fallon, Kodak's CEO, and we came to know each other well, albeit informally. This was near the end of my tenure, and, while I could have parlayed these fortuitous encounters into a meaningful career there, I was at the end of my rope with Kodak. I didn't have the strength, acumen, or interest in using this entrée to further my career at Kodak.

However, I did in fact have an exit interview with Mr. Fallon when I left the company.

In the sales promotion role, I got to travel throughout the country. I generally lived the lifestyle routinely afforded most corporate executives. This mostly came from my creating my own opportunities and the management's leaving me unchallenged. After all, I had been given *carte blanche* to "make the job whatever I wanted it to be."

I ultimately managed a $10 million budget with discretionary control over $7 million of that amount. I was able to give contracts to minority vendors, even before this became "fashionable."

One such person was John Burrell who owned a box manufacturing company. I hired him to produce a promotional and shipping package for a camera kit which was used as a door prize for the Ebony Fashion Fair. I saw John about a year after I had left Kodak; he told me that his contract had been cancelled on the very day that I left the company. This happened even though he'd hired a White guy as his "front man" just to avoid that fate.

During the time that I worked in the Consumer Products Division and before I became enmeshed with sales promotion, I tried for a position within the international division. With my prior successful foreign assignments, I had a real desire to work outside of the United States. I had several good conversations via telephone with the Director of the Middle East, Africa and Asian Division.

He requested my resume, which I sent, he indicated that he liked it. After his review, he personally called and scheduled an appointment for us to discuss the opportunity in person. When I arrived at his office, as soon as he saw me, his face registered shock, he did not offer me a seat; in fact, he did not come from behind his desk, and he immediately said that he no longer had any positions available.

I appealed this action to Phillip Samper who was the Executive Vice President of Marketing for the entire company. I had met and worked with Phil in Puerto Rico where he had served as general manager and had received high praise from him for the quality of my work. Based on this prior experience I expected him to intervene on my behalf but Phil did nothing, so I stayed in the sales promotion area.

The major accomplishment of my time in sales promotion for Kodak was that I managed the introduction of a major new product, Kodacolor 400® Film. I created and directed the entire sales promotion process for the launch. This promotional project cost over $1.5 million and resulted in first year sales for this new product in excess of $400 million.

Another benefit which accrued from this project went to the major advertising agency, Young and Rubicam. Y&R ultimately became the agency of record for the Eastman Kodak Company, supplanting the J. Walter Thompson Agency which had been Kodak's advertising agency since its earliest days.

This change came about after I left the company, I had started the shift by electing to use a local advertising firm, Hutchins Advertising to design the promotional concepts for the Kodacolor 400® film project. Young and Rubicam purchased the Hutchins Agency in 1977 partially on the strength of this project, which gave them an entrée into Kodak.

At the time my decision was considered quite audacious; I took quite a bit of heat from management for using the Hutchins Firm, but I was willing to do it because I remembered J.

Walter Thompson's treatment of me 10 years earlier, when I had applied for a job with them.

During this period, I managed to forge relationships with many people outside the company. One of the best was with George Jackson, who worked in public relations for American Airlines. George was one of the most creative people that I ever met I would say that he was a marketing genius.

George introduced me to people in the business world, entertainment and politics. He and I became very good personal friends. Through my relationship with George, I learned how not to be frustrated with things as they were but to use "the system" to my advantage. We were not only good friends but great business partners, and we worked together on many joint promotions for American Airlines and Kodak. This included the annual Ebony and Jet Magazine Celebrity Tennis Tournaments, held during my three years of involvement in Los Angeles, Washington DC, and Tucson. The Washington tournament (1976) was held in conjunction with the Congressional Black Caucus weekend.

George and I jointly sponsored a portion of the Ebony Fashion Fair. I was instrumental in placing numerous advertisements for Kodak Products in Ebony and Jet Magazines, as well as other Black publications. Notably, I helped secure a major advertising deal for the Amalgamated

Publishers Association, which was the national Black newspapers' consortium for advertising. As a result, I was invited to dinner with the association president, John Procope, Publisher of the New York Amsterdam News and Jennifer Davis, who was one of the primary salespersons for Amalgamated Publishers.

On one occasion near the end of my tenure with Kodak, I visited the headquarters of the Johnson Publishing Company in Chicago, and got to meet Mr. John Johnson. This occurred during a meeting of the Photographic Marketing Association of America's (PMA) convention in August of 1976. Most Kodak Executives attended this meeting of the premier association of the photographic industry, held annually at the Conrad Hilton and the Palmer House hotels in Chicago.

George Jackson had arranged this meeting for me. I'd invited three of my White colleagues to join me but, at the last minute, all of them declined, citing other obligations, so I went alone.

I was met by Mr. Robert Fentress, VP of Advertising at Johnson Publishing who expressed disappointment that none of my White colleagues had come with me. Nevertheless, he took me on a tour of the building, which was impressive and was, maybe still is, the only Black- owned office building on the Chicago Loop.

When we went to meet John H. Johnson himself, Fentress commented that none of the White people came on the tour but "sent the Black guy". Mr. Johnson, ever gracious and astute, said, "One Black man is sufficient to represent three White men any day."

We laughed, made some small talk and I departed. I made sure to inform Mr. Fentress that I was responsible for the significant increase in advertising in their publications and that he could check with his New York salespeople to verify my claim. From that day forward, Mr. Fentress became a raving fan.

This was another period of rather significant transition for me. My marriage to Alice was breaking up and finally ended in divorce in early 1974 after 12 years. Gregory was six years old and Jefferson was one.

I met another lady, Delores and we began to live together, and later marry. I acquired three step children in this process. Jason and Lisa, whom I consider my own children to this day, were 7 and 12 years old, respectively. Alfred Jr. was 17 and on his way out. But that's another story for a different time.

I received help from various sources during this period. The most significant was for the purchase of a house on Claiborne Road in Brighton, one of Rochester's toniest suburbs. This happened because one Sunday afternoon we were driving through a very exclusive neighborhood, as many people used to do on Sunday afternoons.

We passed a beautiful white three-story colonial house with a "For Sale" sign out front. It said BY APPOINTMENT ONLY, so I stopped to make an appointment. Delores was absolutely petrified by the fact that I was so audacious as to approach a house that I obviously knew that I could not afford and ask for an appointment to preview the property.

The gracious owner, Bikki Learner, invited us in on the spot and showed us the property. This was truly a magnificent home; the place had five bedrooms, three and one-half baths and an in-ground heated swimming pool, plus other amenities

We knew there was no way that I could afford that house and I am especially sure that Bikki was aware of that fact. We thanked her for her hospitality and continued on our Sunday afternoon tour of the neighborhood.

This turned out to be another one of the defining moments of my life.

Later that evening I got a call from Bikki's real estate agent, David Silverberg. He asked to come by and talk to us about the house. I told him not to waste his time because we had just been sightseeing and I could not afford to buy that house which was listed for $81,000 (equivalent to $383,000 today). He said he understood but he wanted to talk anyway. I insisted it would be a complete waste of both of our times. He insisted that Bikki had called him and said he was to do whatever was necessary for us to have that house. He told me he was coming over.

When he arrived, I said again that I couldn't afford it. He repeated Bikki's demand that he make it happen. In fact, David let me know he was not leaving until he had a deal, and that I had to make an offer. Ever audacious, I finally said, "If she really wants us to have the house, why doesn't she just give it to us?"

He assured me that was not going to happen, but that I should make an offer for whatever I thought I could afford and he would take it from there. I offered $40,000, I felt I could afford that amount. He countered with $50,000, indicating that he needed to make some money on the deal. I told him that, if she would agree to take a second mortgage for the additional $10,000, we could make it work. That was the deal that she accepted.

We moved into the Claiborne Road residence. Our neighbors were Mr. and Mrs. Gerald Sturman, (He was senior partner of one of Rochester's largest law firms) and Dr. and Mrs. Arthur Moss, head of cardiology at the University of Rochester

Hospital. Two Kodak vice presidents lived across the street, Tom McGrath, who had retired as Vice President of Distribution, and Fred Sawyer, Vice President of Imaging Products. McGrath and Sawyer both moved within three months of our moving into our new house.

One of the great achievements of my career, for which I received neither credit nor reward, is the development of the 24-exposure roll of film. During the four years I worked in sales promotion for Kodak film, I suggested on several occasions that the company convert the standard 20- exposure roll of film to a 24-exposure roll to maintain uniformity in the packaging of the product and gain a sales advantage.

At the time, film was sold in rolls of 12, 20, and 36 exposures, so it seemed perfectly logical to me that it should be 12, 24 and 36 exposure rolls. To change the product packaging would have required only a minimal expenditure and the incremental profit margin would have been huge, in addition to the tremendous promotional coup. However the idea was consistently rejected and management told me on more than one occasion that it couldn't be done. I think it was because the "Black Guy" proposed it.

Kodak had a long standing policy of rewarding employees who originated unique and profitable ideas by allowing them to share in the profits generated from their ideas. This particular idea would have been "off the chain" profitable, but unfortunately no benefit accrued to me.

After I left Kodak, I had an interview, arranged by a recruiter, with Carl Chapman, then president of Fuji Film USA. While I felt that he had no intention of offering me a job and I probably would not have accepted had one been offered, I gave him the idea for the 24-exposure roll. Regrettably, I did not ask for money in exchange for the idea and the rest is history. Within the year, Fujifilm adopted the idea and went on to gain significant market share in the USA for photographic film.

Shortly after my meeting with Mr. Chapman, I started working for Ernest Gallo.

To sell our house, we went back to David Silverberg, who'd brokered our purchase from Mrs. Lerner. David convinced us to list the house for $81,000, the listed price three years earlier. I believe that it was priced well below the market value because we received three bids within the first two weeks.

We were real estate novices and we allowed the house to be sold for that price mostly because we didn't know how the game worked. We did not maximize the profit that should have been realized on the sale of the property.

In any event, we made a profit of over $30,000, (which is equivalent to $173,000 in 2014) and this launched me into the next phase of my life in great financial shape.

CHAPTER NINE

E & J Gallo Winery: The Miracle Years

How I got to California is a miracle story in and of itself. In January 1977, a snow storm hit Rochester, the largest I'd experienced in the 10 years I'd lived there. It snowed 26 inches in a 24-hour period.

The following morning as I looked out of an upstairs bedroom window, I said, "This weather never really bothered me that much before, but this is the straw that broke the camel's back." I'd had enough of the snow and I didn't intend to spend another winter in Rochester.

Delores asked, "Where do you think we're going?"

I answered, "We are moving to California."

Within an hour, a recruiter called. He asked, "How would you like to live in California?" I didn't believe that the call was real so he had to convince me that he was not joking.

I let him know I was interested and that I was already scheduled be in San Diego for a sales meeting. I hadn't been able to leave yet because of the weather. But I would be happy to meet with his client as soon as I could get there, plus I would save them the cost of a plane ticket.

He asked me if I'd like to know who the client was. I told him that it didn't matter. I shared the conversation I had with my wife not more than an hour before his call. We had a good laugh and decided that the call was certainly providential. Then he told me that the client was the E&J Gallo Winery.

I went to the Kodak sales meeting in San Diego for two days, then arranged a flight to San Francisco, rented a car and drove to Modesto, California to meet with Walter Bregman, Vice President of Marketing and Albion Fenderson Executive Vice President of the E&J Gallo Winery for an interview. We met and talked for about two hours and went to dinner.

This meeting went very well and I felt really comfortable with both of these gentlemen. Obviously they felt the same because several days after I'd returned to Rochester, I was invited to come back to Modesto to have lunch with Ernest.

Lunch with Ernest Gallo was a very interesting experience, which I discovered afterwards was almost a ritual. Every day that he was in town

Ernest had lunch with an entourage, which almost always consisted of a coterie of his vice presidents and any other invited or special guests.

Usually the special guest was "lunch." On these occasions, always held at a local restaurant, seats were assigned. Protocol never varied; the special guest was always seated across the table facing Ernest, and on that day it was ME.

Walter Bregman sat on my right and Albion Fenderson on my left. The specific purpose of this line up was, of course, to keep me focused and to make sure that I answered Ernest's questions appropriately. I don't remember much of the conversation, but I do remember that the questions came fast and furiously from Ernest and from his sons, Joe and David, who were seated to his right and left, respectively.

Occasionally, another vice president would ask a question, usually in an attempt to be social. I later learned that while Ernest had lunch every day that he was in the office, in the same manner, the people who were invited to lunch changed frequently. It was customary each morning for his secretary to invite people to have lunch with

Ernest. The invitees changed depending on his desire or need to be updated on some phase of the business. Sometimes it was a reward to specific people, and on other occasions it would be so he could get to know an employee better.

Two days following that lunch, which I never got to eat, E&J Gallo Winery offered me a position as a Marketing (Brand) Manager.

I could hardly contain my excitement at the prospect of finally escaping the environment of Rochester and Kodak. The last trip I took for Kodak was to the Photo Marketing Association meeting in Chicago, February 1977. At O'Hare on my return, an American Airlines customer service agent encountered me and asked why I looked so happy. I told her that I was elated to be going home to give my two weeks' notice the following morning.

The Pacific Regional Manager at Kodak who torpedoed my career 5 years earlier was still in the same job and, as far as I know, retired in it. The man hired in my place as district manager stayed in Seattle and continued in that position for the remainder of my tenure at Kodak.

I started work at Gallo on March 1, 1977. My family stayed in Rochester so the kids could finish out the school year.

I commuted weekly from Rochester for the first four months. My experience at Gallo provided me with the opportunity to really see how White America really lived.

Gallo hired me for $35,000 to start. My final salary at Kodak had been $21,000. After ten years, I was still on the nonexempt payroll even as I directed sales promotions for all of Kodak Film for the US and Canada.

The Gallo salary came with the promise of consideration for a $5000 increase within one year. I had asked for and was given permission to attend and represent Gallo as a sponsor for both the NAACP and National Urban League Conventions annually. I thought that I had won the lottery, but what I later found was that I was just being paid at the fair market rate for my talent and experience. For the first time in my life, I was able to support my family on my income alone. I was, indeed, a happy man.

We made several house hunting trips to Modesto, California. We experienced some housing discrimination again, but we were initially unaware of it. During one visit we put an offer on a house, which was under construction, and were told that it had already sold, which turned out to be a lie. We discovered this about 6 months later when we visited the place again during an open house.

We ultimately bought a house in one of Modesto's upscale neighborhoods. In fact, we discovered soon after moving in that David Gallo lived about six doors away. The fact that he lived in the neighborhood benefited us greatly some time later. We came home one Saturday afternoon and discovered that a vandal had attempted to drain our swimming pool. One night an attempted burglary triggered our alarm. Following these two incidents, Gallo security, which maintained a close watch on David Gallo's residence, also guarded our house for the two years we were in California

The home buying process for our new home in California was remarkable to say the least. The Bregmans gave a party where we were introduced to a bank president as new to the city and in the process of looking for a mortgage.

He invited us to stop by his office on a Monday. Upon our arrival, he greeted us personally and introduced us to a vice president, Al Aguirre, with instructions to "take care of these folks." Al took our mortgage application, opened a checking account, arranged for the new mortgage to be deducted directly from our account and processed a "bridge loan" because the house in Rochester wasn't due to close until July.

He also processed two check guarantee cards for us. In this era before ATM machines, having a check guarantee card was a big deal. We left the bank at the conclusion of our business that morning and never had another direct interaction with anyone about buying our house until our real estate agent brought the paperwork after we'd moved in.

I was supposed to spend my first four months, working from the New York City Regional Sales office, which was managed by George Frank, a long-time Gallo employee. First, I was to travel for a week with the rep covering western New York. I traveled with this man and the local salesperson from the distributor's office in Buffalo for exactly one day. At the end of the day George Frank called, first to congratulate me and then to tell me to report to Modesto within two days.

My first day working with Gallo was very interesting in that it gave me the opportunity to observe some apparent jealousy and animosity on the part of the Gallo Sales Rep. which I didn't understand. I surmise that he felt as if he was being surpassed by a person of color and he didn't like it. The distributor's sales rep did not exhibit anything but friendliness, the Gallo employee was unfriendly and aloof during the entire day. At the end of the day, he was running late for the plane to his next assignment. Instead of being concerned about catching his flight on time, he insisted that the driver drop me off at home before going on to the airport.

Both the driver and I indicated it would be better to take him to the airport first. I sensed that he wanted to see where I lived, mainly because the driver had picked me up at home and had talked about my house during the day. When we arrived at my house, the children were playing in the yard and driveway. He appeared shocked and expressed disbelief. I assured him that it was indeed my house, got out of the car and never heard from him again in any capacity.

I traveled to Modesto two days later to start my new assignment as a brand manager for The E&J Gallo Winery. My supervisor was Assistant Marketing Director Lynn Jordan, a nice enough gentlemen who also never offered any real training or direction about how to do the job, as a result it felt much like my experience at Kodak. I had come to feel that this was typical of corporate America.

If it is not, then it lends credence to my opinion that it is covertly racist behavior.

Some, Whites either consciously or unconsciously do not want to help a Black person get the skills needed to do his/her job.

During my stay at Gallo, I felt that for the first time in my life I was treated as an equal and producing member of the team. My initial position was as Marketing (Brand) Manager for a low- end wine brand called *Flambeau,* designed specifically for the New Orleans market.

I worked in Lynn's department for six months without any specific responsibility beyond Flambeau, which the company chose to discontinue shortly after my arrival. My job consisted of conducting retail surveys of the various markets. Eventually, I learned that surveying a market is a unique skill, one I'd never learned and not one for which I was particularly well suited.

I was one of Gallo's three Black brand managers, along with S. Edward Rutland and Octavia Myles. Ed was a graduate of Morehouse and the Chicago School of Business and managed the "Black" brands, which included Thunderbird and Night Train. Octavia a graduate of UCLA managed the Boones Farm brand.

At the time, the three of us probably constituted the largest percentage assemblage of Black managers at a major corporation in America.

Gallo had 10 brand managers and for 30 percent of this group to be Black was almost unheard of in the corporate world in 1977. The $5000 raise I'd negotiated came through after six months of satisfactory work. At six months I was also promoted to Brand Manager for E&J

Brandy, a major new product and the company's first distilled spirit. I reported directly to J. Peter Conway, Senior Vice President of the Distilled Spirits Division.

The value of this promotion was immediately apparent to me; all of a sudden I was promoted to a significant corporate position and paid a salary of $40,000 annually (equivalent to $200,000 today.) In 1978 this was an astonishing salary for a Black man in Corporate America.

Working with Peter Conway was a great experience. I felt I'd acquired a mentor. He made sure that I was given every opportunity to learn the business and learn the things required to make the job successful. I learned to do retail surveys properly and was responsible for almost every decision regarding the development and promotion of the E&J Brandy brand.

This product was important to the future of the company. While Peter was the ultimate arbiter, I was the brand manager.

Many times he invited me to his office just to listen to conference calls with advertising and sales people. Sometimes when things had gone awry, the sales or advertising manager, who had actually screwed up, would blame me. Not knowing I was listening in, they frequently used racial slurs.

Pete let them talk, and we'd discuss the issue afterwards. Both of us knew full well prior to the call what had happened. We predicted that they would resort to using racial slurs as well as their attempts to divert the blame to me. I came to see American racism at its most sublime.

While at Gallo, I made friends and developed several business relationship, which were beneficial later. As the brand manager, I worked very closely with the advertising department, particularly since we bought a lot of advertising space. In California, the principal advertising vehicle for Brandy was billboards, and I developed a good working relationship with the outdoor advertising salespeople.

One day, I received a call from one of the reps whom I worked with fairly frequently. He invited me to lunch at a downtown restaurant. This was unusual because we mostly ate lunch at restaurants near the office. During the meal, he offered me a new car, which came as quite a shock. I declined, first because I felt it was improper (a bribe, in fact) and second because I wasn't really sure I wasn't being set up. This didn't happen again, but there were other opportunities which I didn't take, but it did make me aware, once again, of the way that White people work in America to get business.

One thing that I did get were tickets to the 1980 Super Bowl Game in Los Angeles through the advertising department. My wife and I were guests of *Sports Illustrated* for the game between the Steelers and the Rams. We also attended a small reception at the Bel Air Hotel on the evening before the game.

This affair was followed by dinner at an upscale restaurant. When we arrived at the reception, we among some 20 people who seemed to be what's now known as the 1 percenters. *One man, whom I noticed shortly after we entered the room, stared at us for about 15 minutes. I began to feel uncomfortable, but before I could ask him why he was staring, he approached and looked directly into my eyes as he asked,* **"How did you get here?"**

I was somewhat startled and I didn't answer right away, he seemed irritated and asked again in a somewhat demanding voice **"How did you get here?"** *I feigned a puzzled look, and answered* **"I drove, how did you get here?"**

The fact that he felt bold enough to ask the question which was probably on the minds of most of the other guests, started my wheels turning. It occurred to me that I was in a circle that had probably never been penetrated by Black Americans before and surely none had penetrated any of the questioner's circles.

Neither of us introduced ourselves so I never knew his name (not that I would have benefited from knowing his name). I do remember one attendee, the subsequent dinner speaker, Peter Ueberroth, President of the 1980 Los Angeles Olympic Committee and later commissioner of major league baseball. Also an elderly gentlemen, and his wife, who said he was the US importer of all of the Toyota automobiles sold east of the Mississippi River.

My job at Gallo was wonderful and I was on the verge of achieving the dream that I had so long harbored; to rise to the upper ranks of Corporate America.

Modesto in 1980 was a city of about 100,000 population with about 3,000 Black People. In fact, my daughter was the only Black person in her high school of 3,500. This ratio troubled my wife who consequently pressured me to leave California.

She had not wanted to leave Rochester in the first place, but I had insisted and in the process, to get her to move, I told her that that I would only commit to staying in California for two years. A decision which I regret until this day.

My managers at Gallo probably sensed the problem I was facing at home regarding staying at the company because Albion Fenderson, the Executive Vice President, took me to lunch one day and said point blank, "We want you to stay," and proceeded to ask what it would take for me to remain.

Working with Peter Conway at Gallo made me realize the importance of having a strong mentor and how much this seemingly simple thing means.

I never got to thank him for the time that I got to spend with him, his guidance shaped my outlook on work and life in general. I feel genuinely sorry that I never took the time to share my feelings with him.

I also realize it is vitally important that the people who want to help be in a sufficiently elevated position to help. Otherwise the assistance is futile. I believe that we need mentors throughout our lives, not just in the early stages.

In later life, we tend to call this networking but the purpose is the same -- to broaden our range of contacts and to find new people who are willing to form relationships with us and with whom we can contribute to each other's mutual success.

My personal belief is that many White people have become so imbued with the thought of racial superiority that the idea of helping a person from a different racial background is completely foreign to their thought process. I don't think that this is entirely conscious, but is part of a larger and subtlety designed strategy designed to maintain a perceived status.

This thinking becomes quite evident in many discussions with Whites today. In random conversations one will often hear comments like, "Things are better now," which is usually based on the fact that a few Black people are now present in the circles in which they travel. The comment is even more common now that a Black man has been elected president of the United States.

I believe that a large number of Black Americans, especially those people living on the margins of society feel that the task of living and achieving a place of significance in this society has become increasingly more difficult. As the national economy has moved from one emphasizing the production of material good to one where the financial and technical arenas are front and center, many Black Americans are becoming less involved and increasingly marginalized.

Additionally, as the demographic makeup of the country shifts, the resources devoted to helping people achieve from almost every perspective are being diverted by the white political structure to maintain the status quo. I don't believe this is a sustainable policy.

In any event, at my stage of life I still believe it is possible for a person to achieve their dreams based on the strength of their tenacity and desire.

CHAPTER TEN

From Wine to Beauty

I had never lived in the South as an adult. As a child, Atlanta, and indeed all of Georgia, was considered to be still mired in slavery and repression by the people whom I knew.

In the early 1980's Atlanta's reputation was on the rise and the city served as a beacon of hope the "New South" for Black Americans I really didn't want to move to Atlanta; I preferred instead to look to New York or Chicago for putting down new roots, but my wife wanted to move to a "Black City." Her reasoning escapes me to this day. I suggested that we try Oakland, but she insisted that we leave California altogether.

My reputation as the Brand Manager for E&J Brandy, which, by that time, was making significant inroads into the marketplace, preceded me.

As a result I was recruited by Glenmore Distillers and ultimately offered an opportunity to move to Louisville, Kentucky.

I interviewed with the Glenmore managers in Los Angeles. Following this meeting, my wife and I were invited to Louisville for further meetings and to look around. I had been in Louisville once, for a meeting of the NAACP about a year earlier, and encountered several people from my college years. One was Robert Tennin, who was in charge of economic development for the City of Louisville.

While in Louisville, we met several times with Glenmore people, visited with my friends and looked for housing. During lunch, on the second day of our visit, I developed a headache. I left the restaurant for a nearby pharmacy to get some aspirin. While walking through the parking lot, a lady in a large dark blue Cadillac almost ran me over. I literally had to jump out of the way. She parked her car, looked at me, sneered and walked toward the restaurant.

I went on for the aspirin; the near miss made the headache a little worse. When I rejoined the group for lunch, the Cadillac woman was sitting at the table. I think she was just as shocked as I was when I approached the table. She was the wife of Glenmore's Chief Marketing Officer. That incident plus the fact that the Glenmore offer of

$35,000, which was $5,000 below my Gallo salary caused me to decline their offer.

I received a call the following Sunday morning from the Glenmore president, asking me to reconsider. He made sure I knew that he was in Paris, staying at the George V Hotel, one of the most exclusive properties on the planet, while asking me to take a pay cut because $35,000 was "all that they could afford." I was not impressed.

I moved to Atlanta on the strength of my acquaintance with Edward Rutland. Ed and I had been colleagues at Gallo. He had left to become the marketing director for M&M Products Company, a Black-owned hair care products company, founded in Atlanta several years earlier.

Ed, an Atlanta native, was a tremendous help to me. More than anyone, he made our transition to the city as easy as possible. He said that if I ever decided to move to Atlanta and start an advertising agency, which was my plan, that he could guarantee me at least $100,000 worth of business. So I moved to Atlanta and opened The Marketing Forum, Inc., a full service advertising agency.

Moving to Atlanta was very stressful and reacquainted me with how life was for Black Americans. I was not exactly sure what to expect, but I did not expect what happened, and it started with housing.

We made a house hunting trip to Atlanta and put an offer on a new house under construction in Vinings with an asking price of $100,000. We signed the contract with the builder on a Thursday afternoon with the promise of a 40 percent down payment. I was to deposit the earnest money on the following Tuesday.

I went to California over the weekend to get the deposit money. When I returned on Tuesday, my realtor and I learned that the builder had voided the contract because he said I was "late with the deposit." This was obviously not true, but later that day, the manager of a C&S Bank Branch on Roswell Road told me that they would not have granted the mortgage anyway because I didn't have a "regular job," the 40 percent down payment notwithstanding.

My next experience with C&S came a few days later when I tried to open a checking account. I went to a branch managed by an African American whom I had met via the people at M&M Products Company. This branch serviced their business and was their primary banking relationship.

I told the manager that I wanted to open a checking account. Because we'd met earlier, I didn't expect a problem. When he asked what my initial deposit would be, I told him $60,000 in the form of a cashier's check drawn on the Bank of America. He seemed to become visibly terrified and started shaking and sweating.

He refused to open the account. I was completely flabbergasted that he appeared so afraid at the idea of opening my checking account, even though I had a $60,000 cashier's check from one of the largest banks in the country. (Obviously this was before Bank of America acquired C&S.) I had no idea about how to react.

Finally, I was able to open a checking account at the Peachtree Center Branch of the C&S Bank. This branch had a White manager whom I did not know beforehand. While he was somewhat reluctant, he did agree to open the account and over a period of several months we managed to develop a cordial relationship.

Subsequently, we were able to buy a house by assuming the mortgage on a house in Southwest Atlanta from a Delta pilot, who appeared to be escaping the invasion of Blacks into the neighborhood.

This was 1980; the mortgage I assumed had a 14 percent interest rate.

By the fall of 1980 we were settled in Atlanta and beginning a brand new way of life. At the time the M&M Products Company account was considered "the plum" one for the Atlanta advertising community. After five years in business, they were approaching $75,000,000 in sales. Everyone wanted the business. We were the new guys on the block, and felt the extreme competitive pressure to perform and deliver for the client. And we delivered, in a big way.

We worked on a number of small promotional projects for M&M, but our major job for them was managing the product launch for their Sta Sof Fro® Curl Kit. We designed all the creative material for this product except the initial packaging, which had been in process prior to our starting with them.

In bringing this product to market, we produced three television commercials, six radio commercials and six print ads. We also did the marketing display pieces and the collateral materials needed to bring the product to market.

The Curl Kit became a very profitable product for M&M and a source of pride for me because it was the third time that I had managed a successful launch of a consumer product, albeit each time from a different perspective. I was now able to add this to my list along with Kodacolor 400® film and E&J Brandy®.

For our work on the Curl Kit project we won a Communications Excellence in Black Advertising (CEBA) award.

I must admit that I was still a dreamer, expecting my creativity and brain power to take me to the heights of success. I think I intentionally ignored the reality of racism in America or, at the very least, I had refused to believe that I was subject to it. This was about to change is some rather dramatic ways.

While working on the M&M project, I often dealt with a White guy, who was something of a fixture on the Atlanta advertising scene. He was constantly in our offices. He was very helpful in identifying freelancers such as photographers, writers, designers, etc. Of course, he was angling for business, too. He worked as a sales rep for a film production company, Reider Films, owned by Frank Reider who was also the principal producer. We agreed to have Reider films produce the three television and six radio commercials for this project. This person stands out in my memory because, after the M&M project was complete, I asked him for some referrals to other potential clients. His response was, "I don't understand what you do." I was completely blown away. We had just completed a $75,000 project with this guy, which involved extensive collaboration and working together across a range of disciplines, and he didn't understand what we did?

I think what he meant was that he didn't understand how Black people functioned, in spite of the fact that we probably represented one of the largest deals of his career to that point in time. Fortunately, working on this project allowed me to meet two of the most creative designers in the city, Billy Mitchell and Tommy Langley. Billy and Tommy dissolved their partnership a few years afterwards, and Tommy moved away, but Billy and I remain friends and colleagues to this day.

Ed Rutland had taken it upon himself to introduce me to several people whom he felt would be helpful in getting our business off the ground.

One of those persons was Fleetwood Price, the Black person in charge of "Black markets" at the Coca Cola Company. Fleetwood promised to do business with us once we opened the office in Atlanta. However, this was an empty promise. As I got to know Fleetwood better, following our initial months in Atlanta, I discovered that he had absolutely no intention of doing business with us.

We had also been introduced to the long-time advertising manager for Coca Cola, an African American that I thought was approaching retirement. One day he asked to come by our offices, his stated purpose, was to review our capabilities with a view toward doing business with the Coca Cola Company.

He arrived and we discussed our resources. He then surprised us by asking if we would consider adding him to our staff or perhaps forming a partnership. This was a very enticing proposal since we were trying to get established beyond the M&M Products Company, our only account at the time.

M&M was a significant account, our billings amounted to over $1.5 million during the first eighteen months of our coming to Atlanta. Ed Rutland had more than kept his promise and I felt like we were well on our way to the pinnacle of success.

That fellow from Coca Cola, we discovered, had visited our agency under false pretenses; he was scouting our operation before leaving Coke to establish his own agency in partnership with two White guys.

In fact within 30 days of his visit , Ed Rutland was fired as the Marketing Director for M&M Products Company and Fleetwood Price was hired as his replacement. Within a few weeks, Fleetwood came to our offices with a marketing consultant. They began to negotiate the termination of the relationship between M&M Products Company and The Marketing Forum, Inc. We were fired, and the account was formally awarded to the former Coca Cola Advertising Manager and his two White associates.

Working with M&M Products Company opened my eyes to a whole new universe of experiences. It allowed me to work with White people, some of whom were genuinely trying to be helpful, friendly, and generous and at least one of whom appeared to an absolute snake in the grass.

Conversely, it allowed me to experience for the first time in my life, Black people telling me directly, "It doesn't matter what your qualifications are. I will not do business with you because I don't do business with Black people." The first person to make this statement to me was a cousin of Atlanta's former mayor, Maynard Jackson. I will never forget that encounter.

The Marketing Forum, Inc. went out of business in 1982. But in spite of it all, we had a very good run. For about two years we had gross sales of almost $1.75 million during our brief tenure and net profits of almost $300,000, we provided employment for 11 people at our peak and made some good and lasting friendships. Life was good for a brief and shining moment.

Near the end of 1981, I became very sick, suffering from a severe depression, a result of side effects from beta blockers in a medication for hypertension. I had begun to suffer from hypertension shortly before I went to California and the problem had been easily controlled. When I moved to Atlanta, my new physician decided that I needed to try a new medication and prescribed a beta blocker which was apparently a new class of drugs.

That experience led me to discover that I am allergic to most medications. I had never taken prescription medications prior to that time, and I was unaware of this condition. As a result, I was hospitalized for two weeks near the end of 1981.

I recognized after the fact that many of the problems which I experienced during this time arose from the depression brought on by my reaction to the medication. I had reached a very low point, and fortunately I haven't been there since.

During this time my marriage to Delores, which was never the best, turned really sour, primarily because I was having an affair with a White woman, who was quite the gold digger. She was an agent with John Hancock Insurance Company. She had approached me initially to sell some life insurance, but then decided perhaps that I was a better target for other activities.

While the advertising agency was doing great, she turned up the charms and I responded in kind. Our marriage suffered to the point where we separated for a while. The affair ended with my hospitalization, but the other problems continued to mount.

On the day that I was released from the hospital, my wife had an accident while coming to pick me up. She totaled my new sports car (She later admitted it was intentional.) and injured her legs. We were both laid up for several weeks; by this time the business was completely gone. My savings meant we were not destitute immediately.

From April 1980 to November 1981 the business grossed about $1.75 million. I went into the hospital in December of 1981, and during the year 1982, my gross income was $7200, mostly from unemployment compensation. From January 1982 until March 1983, I had no regular source of income

I did manage to survive with freelance jobs from several people at The Coca Cola Company. This helped tremendously during this period. I managed to subcontract the graphic design work to a White artist, who worked for the Atlanta Journal Constitution. He would artistically render storyboards based on my creative concepts and designs; he was a talented illustrator but didn't have much independent creative ability.

Our partnership worked well for a while, I paid him $800 for each design that he completed and resold the renderings to Coca Cola for $1600. He always asked how much money I was making off each project, rather than focusing on the amount that he was earning.

I told him that I sold each project for $950.00 so he wouldn't know my income, which in fact was none of his business. It soon became obvious that his interest was not so much in earning money, which he could not have possibly made on his own, as making sure that I wasn't benefiting too much from his labor. This thinking, has always been a puzzle to me. If I agree to do a job for a price, then I am not concerned about what happens to the work after the job is delivered? I am unable to understand this line of reasoning.

I am not really sure if it was racism on his part or just plain jealousy. After several months he stopped doing the work for me, and because I was unable to locate another artist I had to give up the freelance jobs.

The Marketing Forum, Inc. went bankrupt in early 1982, and by the end of 1982 I strongly considered personal bankruptcy in order to forestall foreclosure on our house which we had been unable to sell. The real estate market in southwest Atlanta was nearly dead.

I didn't realize it at the time but filing personal bankruptcy was unnecessary. The mortgage I had assumed was a VA Loan, and I hadn't realized it at the time. The credit problems and reports of late payments did not accrue to my credit but to the prior owner who had taken out the mortgage.

The lender was very cooperative in working with me as I tried to solve my mounting financial problems. At the end of this ordeal we were 18 months past due on the mortgage. I don't know how or why, but we managed to stay in the house until July of 1983.

This is one of the many miracles of my life. I managed to survive this financial turmoil, personal drama with my wife, and the medical drama. During most of this time I was seeing a psychologist regularly. Dr. Allen Carter a wonderful healer who was a tremendous help to me. In fact, I had a very spiritual experience during one session with Dr. Carter.

The turning point in my recovery came one day when I was in a hypnotic state. I had a vision very similar to a "near death" experience. I remember being transported to a place beyond conscious reality and was visited by an angel that I couldn't initially identify. Later, I recognized that it as the spirit of my grandmother, Emma, who died when I was three years old. During that encounter, she promised that I would be OK and that she would be with me through this time of trouble and forever more.

From that day, I have not felt any episodes of depression and I have managed to cope well with most issues. Before that incident, I would get depressed and not be aware of it; I'd start to get listless or have little or no energy for inexplicable reasons. I now recognize these as symptoms of depression. If this happens now, I can usually identify the causes and find ways to deal with them.

In mid-1983, I was at the end of the rope with the house. In June the foreclosure process finally caught up to me. Then another miracle happened: we had been trying to sell the house for months without success.

One night I was sitting in the kitchen and the phone rang. My friend, George Prothro, was calling to ask me if I would consider selling my house. I couldn't believe my ears.

We had that house on the market for over a year with no interest whatsoever. George said that they had just sold their house, out of the blue, to a gentleman who was passing by. The guy spotted their house from the street and stopped in to ask if he could buy it. George, indicated that they had no prior intention to sell their house, but they sold it on the spot, which also meant they didn't have anywhere to live.

During a family conversation, his kids wondered if the Parkers would be willing to sell their house. So George called to ask. He had no idea that we were about to be foreclosed. So I invited him over and told him my story.

I asked him to see the deal through without "holding me up". He could have taken complete advantage of my situation, but he was a man of good character. We worked out terms favorable to both of us. We sold the house and assisted in the financing by taking back a $10,000 second mortgage to help George qualify for the loan.

This saved us from foreclosure, but now we had nowhere to live. On the day we closed I asked George if I could store our furniture in the basement until we could locate a place to move and he agreed.

While the furniture was being moved, I took a break, and went into the backyard to have a conversation with God. I said that I knew that He was sending me a "symbolic" message, but I was not sure just what was being communicated because I was not – and I am still not—fluent in "symbolism". I just wasn't getting it. Nevertheless, I was sure that one day I would understand, just not that day.

At that moment my neighbor Mildred Seagraves, came out to ask me how I was doing. I said matter of factly, "Mildred, I am 40 years old and tonight I don't have anywhere for my family to sleep. We are homeless and I don't even have enough money to rent a hotel room."

She started crying and ran back into the house. I surely didn't expect that reaction but I stayed to continue my conversation with God. At first I thought Mildred was a "sign", but after that response I wasn't quite so sure.

I looked up and said to God again, "I don't understand the message being delivered, but I am sure that I will one day", but I was absolutely sure of one thing, God did not bring me to that time and place to leave me there.

Within a few moments Mildred came back, apologizing for running away. She said that she had called her husband, John, and they agreed that we could stay at their house for as long as we needed. I had experienced another of my life's defining moments.

The next week I managed to sell the $10,000 second mortgage that I had taken back from George for $6000, this money allowed me to pay the Seagraves a debt that they were owed by a nonprofit organization that I was involved with, which had not paid them for prior services, and it allowed me to rent a house in Marietta, Georgia. This was my first foray into East Cobb County, a predominantly White suburban community.

I searched but I was unable to find a job in Atlanta. So I developed a coupon book idea, targeting upscale visitors to Atlanta. I arranged a verbal agreement with the president of the Atlanta Convention and Visitors bureau, who agreed to distribute the book to conventioneers.

I designed the book and started to solicit advertisers. Ads were coming in at a moderately successful rate when the bureau president backed out of the deal. Instead, he decided to produce his own publication called "Atlanta Gold" which I later discovered was modeled on a book of similar design, "Hawaii Gold." His publication failed to catch on, and, after a few months, he was terminated as head of the ACVB. I haven't heard of him since. I saw this as another example of a White guy with little or no creativity, taking advantage of the opportunity to steal from a Black guy without apparent consequence to himself. Now I recognize that some people may not see this incident as racist, but from my perspective, it is a classic example of what has happened to Black people for generations.

CHAPTER ELEVEN

Venture into a New World: Insurance and Financial Services

In February 1983, while making a sales call for that coupon book, I met Roy H. Greene, Jr., a local manager for Phoenix Mutual Life Insurance Co. We met at a very popular luxury rugs and carpet store in Buckhead.

Roy was there with a young agent trying to sell the owner of the store some disability insurance and I was trying to sell an advertising page in my coupon book. Neither of us made a sale, but he invited me to come to his office to talk about a job opportunity. I took him up on the offer and went for the interview.

Phoenix Mutual required potential new agents to complete a qualifying test called a LIMRA Profile, which I took and scored 17 of a possible 20 points, which was one of the highest scores they had seen to that point. They offered me a job, and, since I hadn't had any steady income for almost 18 months, I took it.

I thought I had really lucked out, being hired by Phoenix Mutual. I understood it was a commission-based job but they paid a training allowance of $1300 a month. This was not nearly enough money for my household, but it was steady income.

My first year with Phoenix was successful, I earned National Rookie of the Year honors by leading all first year agents in the company for the year. And I did it working from March through December. That achievement earned me a trip to the Phoenix Sales Conference in Puerto Rico. None of the Black agents that I encountered questioned my success but several of the White agents wanted to know, "How did you do that?" I didn't fully understand their questioning at the time, but later, two different individuals said, they didn't believe that a Black agent could achieve at such a lofty level, especially since there were so few Black people in the business—then or now.

I went on to lead the company in sales for new agents during each of my first two years. Thirty years later I am still working in the business. This has not been an easy career; but my tenacity, ability, and skill have afforded me a very good lifestyle.

Early in my financial services career, I decided to focus my efforts on working with White Americans because, as the notorious bank robber, Willie Sutton, once said when asked why he robbed banks, "That's where the money is."

We had moved to Marietta in the summer of 1983 into a house in a lower working class neighborhood, a far distance physically and psychologically from where we had been. We had lived there for a year when the owner decided that he wanted to sell the house. He was asking $100,000. We didn't want to buy this house because we knew its problems so we decided to move. This was the beginning of yet another miracle.

In June 1984, we were looking for another house to rent. After looking for several days we could find nothing in the school district we desired. I decided to change strategy. When my wife asked what the new strategy would be, I told her we were not going to rent a house but that we were going to buy a house. She thought I'd lost my mind.

We had no savings and not much income but I was determined. She accepted my decision, and we proceeded to look for a house to purchase. We found one in a nearby neighborhood and made an offer. The offer was accepted, but I was not approved for a mortgage.

Undaunted, we continued the search. After several more days, I changed the strategy again. We'd been looking at previously owned houses, I said going forward, that we would only look at newly constructed houses.

I'd never lived in a new house and, I think, I was over having to clean any more toilets. We started looking only for new houses. A few weeks later my wife called to tell me that she had found the perfect house in a new subdivision under construction. She contacted the real estate agent to arrange a walk-through.

The framing was completed, but not much beyond that point. We toured the construction site with the agent, and I agreed with my wife that we liked the property. The asking price was $89,000, which was within our reach. During this process, the owner of our rental house decided to attempt to evict us for "interference with his ability to sell his property."

He took us to court in June. While he didn't achieve the eviction that he sought, the judge told us that we had to move within 90 days or by September 15, 1984. I specifically mention this date because that date was the start of another miracle in my life. We told the builder of this court decision, which was putting stress on our contractual move-in time. The builder agreed to meet that target date so we could move in on schedule.

My financial situation had changed, but not that much, and I still thought I had a foreclosure record on my credit report. With a regular source of income, however, I was able to obtain financing for the new house. This was when I learned that there was no foreclosure record in my name. It had been charged to the prior owner from whom we had assumed the mortgage.

On September 15th, the scheduled date of our move, the new house was not completed. The builder had some final issues and needed another week to finish the house. We could not wait past the September 15th date due to the legal judgment. That's when the miracles started again. The builder allowed us to move into the house one week prior to closing.

Financing had been arranged, but I needed to have $12,500 in cash to complete the deal. On the day of closing, I had only $7500.00. This was $5000 short of the amount needed. The closing was scheduled for 10 AM at the attorney's office.

At 9 AM I was standing at the end of the driveway and the builder drove up and asked "how are you doing?"

I replied,

"Oh just fine"

I think he sensed a little trepidation, so then he asked, "Well how am I doing?"

I responded "probably not too well."

I explained that I was $5000 short for the closing which was scheduled in only one hour.

And that I had no idea how I was going to raise the money.

The builder's response was, "Wait right here."

Just prior to his arrival, I had been engaged in another of my "conversations with God." The conversation went this way, "God, here I am again, in need of a real blessing and I have no idea where it's coming from. But like I said before, I know you did not bring me to this place to leave me. Please provide an answer."

In 10 minutes, his business partner drove up with a personal check for $5000. We agreed it would be a 90-day loan and drafted an agreement on a legal pad on the back of her car.

I went to the closing with all the needed money. I recognize this as another of my life's defining moments.

I was able to repay the loan within the 90 day. I sold the builder and his partner some life insurance, which helped me to defray the costs.

We lived in that house for 10 years, after which we had a house custom built to our specifications for over $300,000.

My insurance sales career really began to take off. By 1985 I had been in the business almost two years, and it seemed the hard struggle stage was about over.

One day I placed a cold call to the R.A. Siegel Company trying to sell group disability insurance and by chance I was put through to the president Mr. Chip Siegel, I asked for an appointment and he agreed to take the meeting. The RA Siegel Company, is an Armstrong Flooring distributor. He didn't buy the disability insurance, but, as I was about to leave, he remarked, "I would buy $1,000,000 of life insurance today if I thought that I could get it."

I stopped cold in my tracks and turned around and asked, "Why do you think that you can't get it?" He invited me back into his office and proceeded to tell me that he believed he was uninsurable because of several pre-existing medical problems.

I telephoned an underwriter from his office and explained the medical conditions that concerned Mr. Siegel. The underwriter said he thought he could issue a $1 Million policy with a 300 percent rating.

I calculated the premium amount and gave Chip the number, and let him know that we could get him insured. I wrote the application and was able to get the life insurance for him issued with a final rating of 250 percent, which was lower than expected. The friendship that began that day lasted 16 years, the remainder of his life.

Meeting Charles H. "Chip" Siegel, became a game-changer for me and my business. He later became a personal friend. In fact, I considered Chip to be my second mentor.

Chip invited me to join the board of The Galloway School, a prestigious private school in Atlanta, from which my youngest son would eventually graduate. He frequently invited us to parties at his house and introduced me to people in his social circle. These introductions did not always result in a business relationship, but Chip always made sure these people were aware of my profession.

One day he asked if I'd consider joining his Rotary club. I had never heard of Rotary but I agreed and I have been a member of the Midtown Atlanta Rotary Club since 1996. I have remained a member because of the friendships and camaraderie that I've developed with members over the years. Being a member has afforded me opportunities to meet people that I would have never met during the ordinary course of things.

I believe that meeting Chip has contributed more than $500,000 in earnings to my career. My journey through the financial services world has had a few not-so-profitable turns over the years too, I realize this is a business where Black People are practically invisible.

After 30 years in this profession, it is still difficult to find Black People thriving in almost any area of the financial services industry. I have achieved life membership status in the Million Dollar Roundtable, the premier sales organization of financial professionals. The MDRT has about 40,000 members worldwide, but the African American membership is less than 1%.

I have managed to achieve success in this business and have been a member of the MDRT for over 28 years even considering its stringent annual qualification process.

During my early years in financial services, there were some difficult moments. One that particularly stands out was with the Eastern Airlines Credit Union in 1985. I agreed to partner with another Phoenix agent to negotiate an agreement to sell insurance in the branches of the Eastern Airlines Credit Union. The deal was initially brought to the table by the other agent, a rookie in the same Phoenix office.

She asked me and we agreed to work jointly on the case, a common practice in the industry. I took the lead position as the more experienced agent but our agreement was to split evenly any revenue that flowed from the deal. As I began working on the case, one of the first requirements was to go to Miami, Florida to meet with several members of the credit union's board of directors and management.

This initial meeting took place in a conference room at the Miami International Airport. The credit union was headquartered in Miami and had a significant presence in Atlanta. This first meeting in Miami was lengthy, but it provided an opportunity for us to get to know each other better and allowed me the chance to understand the desires and objectives of the credit union.

The agreement details were refined at a follow up meeting and later finalized with a series of conference calls. The credit union was in the process of negotiating all kinds of deals with various entities to shore up its services and offerings to members. Insurance seemed to be a perfect fit.

We all agreed we had an acceptable proposal. The final step was to meet in Miami at the credit union's headquarters to sign the final agreement.

I went to Miami for the meeting, which was in a rather impressive conference room on the executive floor of the credit union building. We were waiting for the arrival of

Arthur "Art" Russo, President of the Eastern Airlines Credit Union. After about 15 minutes the door opened and in came a short man wearing a black suit, white shirt and a black tie. His hair dyed jet black. Art stormed into the room at a very quick pace, holding his head down, he apologized for being late.

When he reached the middle of the room, he looked up, spotted me sitting at the table and stopped. He exclaimed, in a very loud voice: "Oh, shit! I didn't know you were Black...No one told me you were Black" Everyone in the room appeared stunned by his outburst.

A bit taken aback, I replied immediately, "What difference does that make?"

He attempted to compose himself and continued to his seat at the conference table. He said, "It doesn't make any difference."

Everyone, however, at the table knew that it made all the difference in the world. The friendly demeanor of the group changed dramatically; the contract, which had been prepared by the credit union's own attorney who was at the table, was never presented.

Some cursory discussion ensued, but after about 30 minutes of everyone trying to recover from his outburst, it was obvious that nothing was going to happen, the meeting disbanded and the deal was never consummated.

I have occasionally looked back on this event, and while I was very disappointed, I've tried to put a good personal spin on it by thinking that some deals fall apart for inexplicable reasons. Later you discover The Universe was more aware of the dangers that lay ahead than you were and kept you from danger.

Eastern Airlines filed for bankruptcy a few months after that meeting. In the ensuing years the Eastern Airlines Credit Union ceased to be a credible or viable organization. It also appears that Mr. Russo went on to make some bad business decisions that ultimately led to the demise of the Eastern Airlines Credit Union.

I make this point here to say that I have sensed a pattern emerging; many organizations that fail, intentionally or unintentionally, to fully appreciate the value added by people of different racial, ethnic, or cultural backgrounds or who practice either conscious or unconscious racism, appear ultimately to meet bad ends. This speaks to my earlier premise that the costs of racism is borne as much by the perpetrator as the intended victim, and often the cost is greater to the perpetrator.

Not having made the deal with the Eastern Airlines Credit Union, was surely another critical moment in my life but definitely one in which God kept me from walking into a disaster from which I might not have recovered.

I later acquired the Georgia Telco Credit Union (currently Georgia's Own Credit Union) as a client. I represented this organization successfully for over 12 years.

Although we worked with many White businesses, I never walked away from doing business with Black firms and individuals. These are my people and the need for financial services in the Black Community is great.

My experiences in Atlanta, however, showed me that it would be difficult to penetrate this market to any great degree. This wasn't always due to a lack of money in the Black Community. I have been told on several occasions by a Black people that they "just didn't do business with other Black people" a concept I still don't quite grasp.

One incident of this occurred in 1997 when I hired a new employee, Jackie Edwards, who had relocated from California. She introduced me to her former employer, a Black woman who had built a very successful home health care business. This lady expressed a desire to sell her company and retire to Atlanta.

We met with her and started to assist her in this endeavor. We brought in a business broker, who happened to be another client of ours to assist with the sale. After several months, during which she consistently failed to provide the documents or information needed to proceed, we ended our efforts and terminated the relationship.

Jackie later told me that her old boss did sell the business but with another resource. She told Jackie that she decided not to deal with my firm because she "couldn't stand the thought of a Black man making that much money off her."

About two years after she sold her business, I asked how she was doing. I was told that she was completely broke and back to working in a job making about $35,000 a year. I was shocked because I felt that she should have netted at least $2 million after taxes on the sale of her business.

I believe that there are people who still live, at least in their minds, in a segregated world and who are still troubled by vestiges of segregation and discrimination - both Black and White.

However, I think about people who harbor these feelings, in much the same way as Harriet Tubman did when asked, about how many slaves she rescued, she responded, "About a thousand, but I could have saved a thousand more if only they had realized that they were slaves."

I remain firmly committed to ensuring the success of Black professionals that I meet, particularly in the financial services business. I make it a priority to mentor and give advice often.

I have served as president of the Atlanta chapter of the National Association of Insurance and Financial Advisors, and president of the Atlanta Chapter of the Society of Financial Service Professionals.

I have served on the national board of directors of the Society of Financial Service Professionals. In this capacity I was instrumental in establishing this group's first affiliation with a college via their University Partners Program at Fayetteville (NC) State University, an HBCU.

I am currently working with the society to initiate a series of seminars, scheduled to roll out nationally, targeting Black, Hispanic, and Asian communities, in an attempt to bring financial education to the people in these communities who are not typically served by mainstream financial services professionals.

CHAPTER TWELVE

The Continuum

Living in Atlanta has been an interesting experience, I came here in 1980 to start life as an entrepreneur. I had significant help and assistance from some wonderful people in getting started on this journey but entrepreneurship was never my desire or intent.

I allowed myself to be talked into becoming an entrepreneur by my then wife. Her father instilled in her the idea of owning your own business and this was her goal. I often encouraged her to start a business but she never did, for reasons which remain unknown. Apparently, being in business vicariously through me was sufficient.

I had always set my sights on rising to the top of a major corporation, this goal was not to be realized at Union Carbide where I started my adult working life. And now, Union Carbide has faded into the annals of history.

At Kodak my career was derailed by a person whom I never met, but of whom I can definitively say was a racist in the vilest sense of the term. His attitude and behavior was tolerated and widely abetted by other people in the company. Today, Kodak is a small shadow of its former iteration.

Rising to the upper echelons of management at the E&J Gallo Winery was a very real possibility, and I am sure that I would have had a wonderful career and a really good life. In fact, at the meeting just two weeks before I left, Albion Fenderson told me they really wanted me to stay at Gallo and would do whatever it took to make sure I had a good career.

I have been a financial advisor for over 30 years now, and while I have had occasion to look back, sometimes wistfully, I do not feel sorry for myself for what I have achieved. I have experienced many effects of racism over the course of my career, but, in spite of it all, I have managed to thrive. Maybe because I was "different," maybe because I always refused to look at the color of my skin as a hindrance, but as a real advantage, because it has allowed me to move in all arenas of society without fear.

For the past 25 years, I have experienced an income consistently in the six figure range, and in some years into seven figures. My successes have allowed me to travel all over the globe, to visit some of the best places on the planet, to send my children to the best schools and to meet some of the best people.

I continue to work every day to meet the challenges of "living while Black" in the United States of America. For those who are not Black it may be impossible to comprehend the extent of the challenge. I think I have managed to cope, and, in many ways, I have overcome the challenges, mainly by keeping the thought at the forefront of my mind, that I am an extremely intelligent and talented person with much to give.

I will stay dedicated to eradicating any vestige of racism that I find, wherever I find it. I may not be the final arbiter but I do believe that a change is in the air and it will come.

Life is never what we expect, but it does go on nonetheless. My life has been a series of really interesting and wonderful experiences. I have encountered and I continue to encounter brilliantly creative Black and White people who are doing wonderful things, and I remain extremely optimistic. In many instances in my life, the lemon has produced succulent lemonade.

My personal mission remains: To make sure that every person whom I encounter, whether in a personal or business relationship, is left better for the experience.

About the Author

A husband, father and mentor, William Parker has over 50 years of experience in corporate America and as an entrepreneur. As an author and businessman, his driving motivation is to always give more than he gets.

For his clients, that means delivering personal, straight-forward advice geared towards each individual's goals and needs. In life, that means giving back to his community through service, education and mentorship.

His debut title, "How Did You Get Here? One Black Man's Journey through White Corporate America" (2015) chronicles his experience from the beginning of his corporate career in 1965 to its end as well as his foray into entrepreneurship.

The journey started with the help of black businessman Richard V. Clarke through his employment agency, Richard Clarke & Associates the nation's first diversity recruitment firm, in New York City. William worked for noted companies such as Union Carbide Corporation, Eastman Kodak Company and E&J Gallo

Winery and provided a game-changing idea to Fujifilm Corporation, a competitor of Kodak.

William has had many successes, most of which were unprecedented for Black Americans His civil rights struggle was against the racism intricately woven into the American Corporate System. This is a problem inherently hard to recognize from the outside, but easy to pinpoint when you are the main target.

William is the founder and president of ABG Financial Services, Inc., he is a life member of the Million Dollar Roundtable, former National Board Member of the Society of Financial Service Professionals, Past President of the Atlanta Chapter of the National Association of Insurance and Financial Advisors, Past President of the Atlanta Chapter of the Society of Financial Service Professionals, member of the Atlanta Estate Planning Council, former Board Member of The Galloway School, a member of Cascade United Methodist Church, Board member of the Atlanta Harm Reduction Coalition, President of the Terrell Mill Community Association, Member of the Cobb County Transportation Advisory Board, and a member of the Midtown Atlanta Rotary Club.

www.howdidyougethere.us

Made in the USA
Charleston, SC
12 April 2015